AF662414

Collins

Digi Tech

4

Manasi Kashikar
Sneha Krishnan

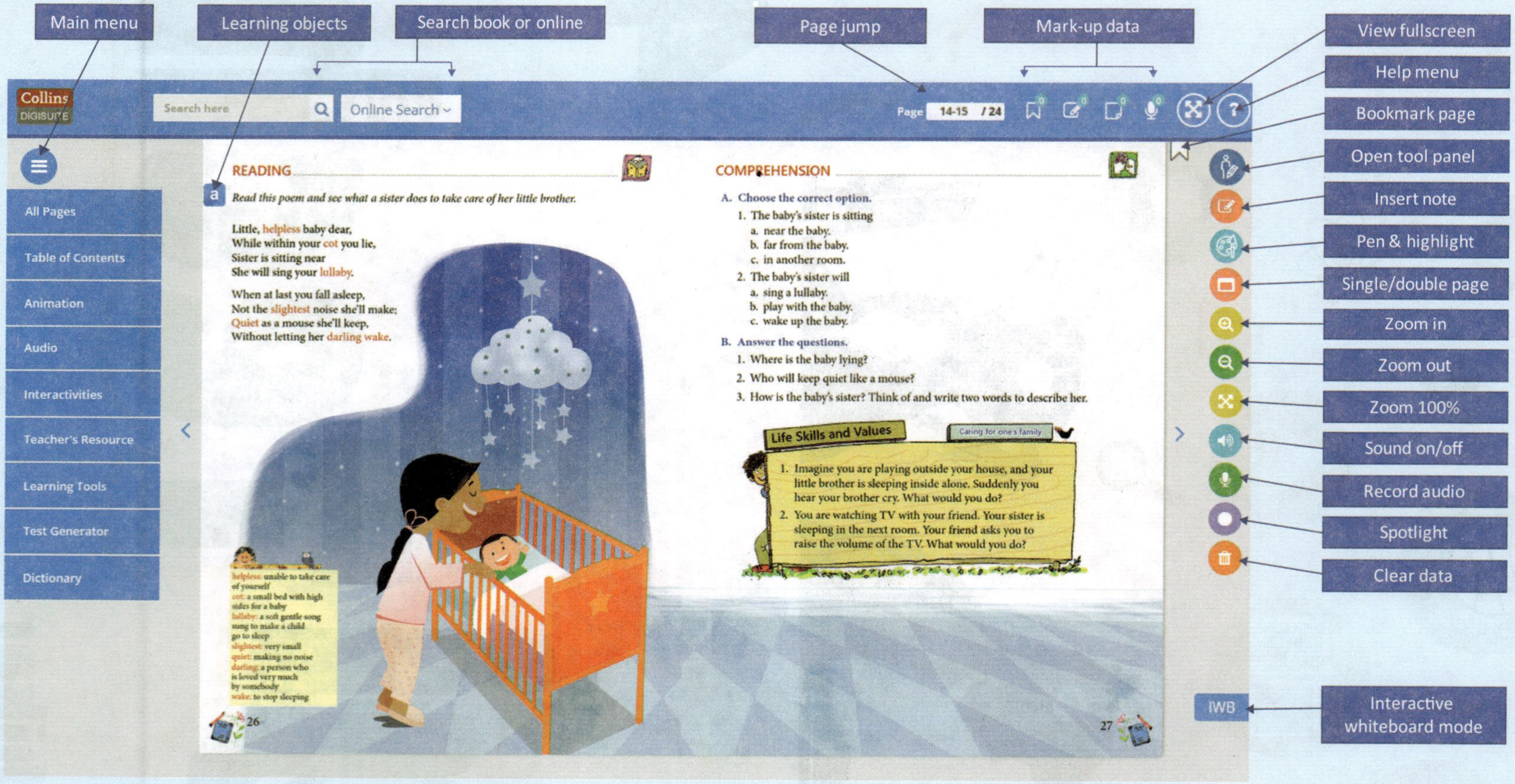

Student + Teacher		Teacher-only	
a animations	**ia** activities	**lp** lesson plans	**tn** teacher's notes
ilt instructor-led tutorials	**w** worksheets	**w** worksheets	**ak** answer keys
g games	**v** videos		
audio			

PREFACE

Over the last few decades, technology has touched almost all aspects of our lives. As technology continues to evolve more rapidly than ever, users are learning newer ways of harnessing the power of technology in their daily lives. In India, easy access to smartphones and affordable internet services have put the power of technology in the hands of millions.

In this backdrop, we believe, it is important for students to:

- ✓ Understand that technology is going to keep evolving. As citizens of the digital world that we all inhabit, keeping abreast of the latest advances is no longer optional, rather, it is an essential life skill.
- ✓ Appreciate that coding skills are as essential today as basic literacy and numeracy. This has been emphasized in the National Educational Policy of 2020 as well.
- ✓ Understand that technology is pervasive and they need to be able to comprehend its intersection with other disciplines. In other words, they need to learn to use technology as a tool to achieve a goal.
- ✓ Take control of regulating their usage and make constructive use of their access to computer devices.

While authoring this series, we have designed and presented the content with the intent of helping students in developing the skills described above. We have ensured that the topics are covered in a relatable manner and that the exercises are practical and applicable. The textbook along with its resources for teachers will enable them to deliver this subject effectively, while keeping the students engaged and interested.

In addition to the curriculum imperatives, we have included concepts as outlined in the National Education Policy 2020. Every grade has computational thinking–based practice problems that are aligned to Bloom's Taxonomy. Topics such as coding and app development have been given their due consideration as their relevance increases in the real world and while making career choices. Artificial intelligence has been woven into the chapters in an age-appropriate manner in the form of Fun with AI boxes, with the intent of enabling students to understand key concepts and applications of AI.

The series equips students with not only the skills required to excel in technology and make the most of it, but also exposes them to the practical applications of these in the world around them.

We would like to thank our intern Sejal Gupta in helping us shape the content.

KEY FEATURES

After reading this chapter, I will be able to:

- ✔ Describe step-by-step thinking.
- ✔ Analyse a task and break it up into parts.
- ✔ Predict the possible solutions.

Well-defined learning objectives that are mapped to the curriculum to help students identify the topics they will read about in the chapter

Activities and discussions based on real-life situations to set the context for what students are about to learn

Information Literacy

Brainstorm and explore!

Riya and her friends are excited for the month of October as mid-term exams end! Look at the calendar for the month of October shown here. Answer the following questions to help Riya and her friends plan their activities for the month.

1. How many days does the month of October have? ____________
2. How many holidays/celebrations are there in the month of October? ____________
3. How many festivals fall on a Sunday? ____________

Soak up!

The process of the operating system loading when a computer is turned on is called booting.

Additional information/facts about the topic being taught

Contextual meaning of difficult words

Windows has a Graphical User Interface (GUI), as shown in Fig. 2.2. This means that it uses picture-like items (the mouse pointer/icons used for folders). Different icons are used for different file types. This makes it the most commonly used operating system. Some of its advantages are given below:

1. It is very easy to use.
2. It works with most software programs.
3. There are many applications and games available for download on the Windows OS.
4. It is the most widely used OS for desktop computers in the world.

Soak up!

Microsoft was founded by Bill Gates and Paul Allen. As of 2020, Satya Nadella, who is of Indian origin, is the CEO of this corporation.

icon: a picture that helps us identify programs on a computer

Tips and shortcut tricks for the topics covered in the chapter to foster inquiry- and discovery-based learning

Technology Literacy

Crank up!

MS Word also gives the option of selecting the word from another language. At the bottom of the Thesaurus task pane, click on a language. Explore this option in the computer lab.

Hands-on tasks for revision, based on the application of the concept taught

Clear up!

Navigate to your favourite image or song file on your computer. Right-click on the file and then select Properties. Did you find the size of the file?

Brush up!

List names of search engines apart from the ones mentioned in the chapter.

____

____

Short questions to reinforce the concept learned and promote competency-based learning

Exemplifies the relevance and application of AI to the concept in the real world

Fun with AI

Data mining is the discipline that finds patterns in large amounts of data. Artificial Intelligence is the tool that is used to aid scientists and programmers to undertake data mining.

Real-world examples and situations to help students establish linkages and connections to support the development of lateral thinking

Link up!

Books and magazines have professional editors who ensure the published material is relevant, accurate and interesting!

Today I learned!

- Breaking down a task into smaller steps and arriving at possible solutions to achieve the desired goal is known as step-wise thinking.
- After dividing a task into simple steps, it is important to follow the steps in an orderly manner. This is called sequential thinking.
- Reasoning and sequential thinking are examples of mental tools we use to effectively solve problems or even deal with simple situations.

Recapitulates all the important points covered in the chapter

Revision exercises comprising a blend of both objective and long-answer questions, including both fact- and application-based questions in a variety of formats

Revise and polish!

Learning Skills

1. Tick (✓) the correct answer.
   a. Which of the following storage devices uses flash memory?
      (i) SD cards ☐ (ii) RAM ☐ (iii) ROM ☐ (iv) Volatile ☐
   b. Which of the following is the fastest way to access data in the primary memory?
      (i) RAM ☐ (ii) ROM ☐
      (iii) Hard disk ☐ (iv) Cables ☐

Lab Activities

Experiential Learning

1. Create a document containing the names of five flowers you have seen in your neighbourhood, school or parks. Change the font colour of each flower name to the colour of the flower.
2. Create a document with the names of the Seven Wonders of the World. Highlight all the seven names with the seven colours of the rainbow.
3. Create a document with two paragraphs describing your favourite game. Highlight the parts you think are important.
4. Using the Thesaurus option in MS Word, find the synonyms of the following words:
   a. Splendid b. Joyous
   c. Moments d. Special
   e. Blessing

Based on the practical application of the concepts taught to enhance comprehension and provide opportunities for peer tutoring

Practical applications of the concepts covered to help analyse and understand real-world situations, with some extra effort put into research and information gathering

Projects

Along with a classmate, create a desktop of the future. Include any applications or features that you think will enhance the utility and look-and-feel of the desktop. Draw and colour the desktop of the future on a chart paper and present it to the class. Remember there are no limits to your imagination!

Competency-based question Computational Thinking

Worksheet 1 (Chapters 1 and 2)

1. Match the following data sets to complete the information.

a.	Search "coding classes in India" on search engine	(i)	001
b.	Find your rank in the class	(ii)	1460 search results with different websites of coding classes in India
c.	Testing blood sample of an individual	(iii)	List of scores of all the students
d.	+91 876510**00	(iv)	Finding the blood group of the individual
e.	M Akshay F Sonam Mahima Pooja	(v)	Calling on +91 876510**00 phone number
f.	1 in binary language	(vi)	Akshay Sonam Mahima Pooja (Grouping individuals on the basis of their gender)

Chapter-based revision worksheets focused on competency-based learning and one dedicated worksheet on developing computational thinking through playing games and problem-solving

NEP IN DIGI TECH

These are some of the key skills that you will see occurring throughout the books at various stages.

21st Century Skills

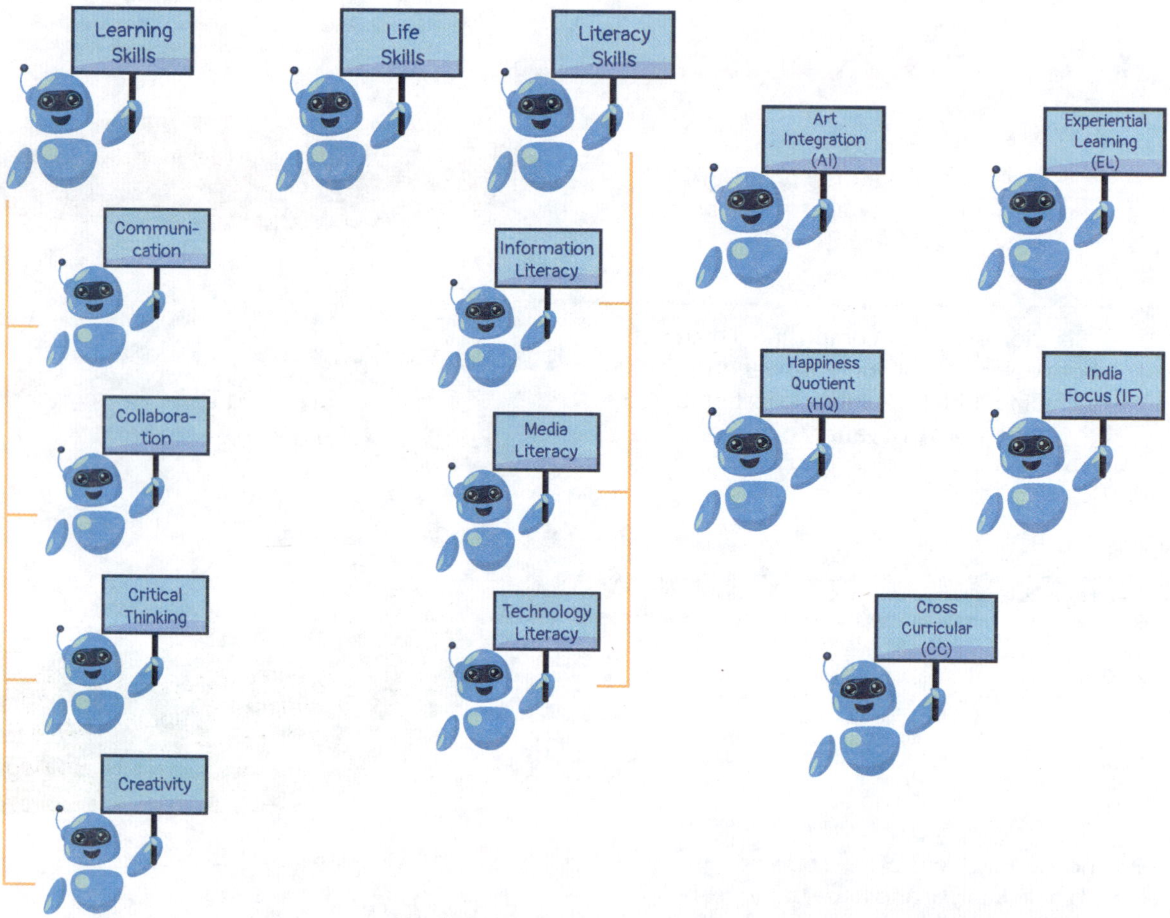

ABOUT THE AUTHORS

Sneha Krishnan and **Manasi Kashikar**, techies at heart, bond over their love of coding. They are co-founders of the company *MindChamp* where they teach coding to school students using fun, activity-based learning. They both love to teach students and that reflects in their work. Together with a team of educators, they have taught thousands of students to create computer games and websites. They want to make coding accessible to young students as well, so they are better equipped for the future.

CONTENTS

Chapter

1

Storage and Memory Devices

After reading this chapter, I will be able to:

- ✔ Differentiate between the terms *data* and *information*.
- ✔ Explain the purpose of internal and external memory.
- ✔ Describe different data storage units.
- ✔ List primary and secondary data storage devices.

Brainstorm and explore!

Riya and her friends are excited for the month of October as mid-term exams end! Look at the calendar for the month of October shown here. Answer the following questions to help Riya and her friends plan their activities for the month.

1. How many days does the month of October have? ____________
2. How many holidays/celebrations are there in the month of October? ____________
3. How many festivals fall on a Sunday? ____________
4. Is the number of Saturdays equal to the number of Sundays? ____________
5. What day is it on the 1st of November? ____________

In this example, we answered all five questions simply by looking at the calendar of the given month. A calendar is nothing but a table that shows the days and weeks in a month. It contains the **data** of dates, days and weeks, which provides us **information** about holidays, festivals, length of the month and so on.

Data and Information

Data and information are important in computing. Data refers to facts, figures and other details stored in a computer. For example, a word document is a collection of words and sentences that can convey a wide range of meanings. A music file is a collection of sounds that come together in a harmonious way to give us a song.

Data is a collection of facts, concepts or instructions.

Information is processed data, on which decisions and actions are based.
Information = Data + Meaning

The terms *data* and *information* are used interchangeably. Table 1.1 shows the differences between data and information.

Table 1.1 | *Differences between data and information*

Data	Information
Collection of facts, unprocessed	Processed data that can be easily understood by humans
Not arranged in any order, may or may not be meaningful	Data that is processed or analysed
May or may not have a specific purpose	Used for decision-making or deriving meaning in a particular situation

Brush up!

Based on the October 2022 calendar shown on the previous page, create two questions and ask a classmate to answer those!

1. ______________________________

2. ______________________________

Fun with AI

Data mining is the discipline that finds patterns in large amounts of data. Artificial Intelligence is the tool that is used to aid scientists and programmers to undertake data mining.

Data Storage Units

A bit is the smallest unit of storage in a computer. It holds the value 1 or 0. In computers, all information is stored and transmitted in the form of electrical signals. A bit with a value 1 represents ON, and a bit that holds a value 0 represents OFF. Eight bits form a byte. Unique sequences of 0 and 1 represent data stored in files. Although they seem simple, the combination of 1 and 0 can be used to make a large number of patterns!

Table 1.2 lists the possible patterns using up to three bits.

Table 1.2 | *Patterns using bits*

Number of bits used	Patterns
One	0
	1
Two	00
	01
	10
	11
Three	000
	001
	010
	011
	100
	101
	110
	111

In the language of machines, 0000 is used to represent the number 0, 0001 is used to represent the number 1, 0010 is used to represent number 2 and so on!

Technology Literacy

Crank up!

List down the different patterns possible with four bits.

____

____

Different units used to measure file sizes are given in Table 1.3.

Table 1.3 | *Units of measurement of file sizes*

Units	Conversion
Bit	Smallest unit of data
Byte	8 bits = 1 byte
Kilobyte (KB)	1024 bytes = 1 kilobyte
Megabyte (MB)	1024 kilobytes = 1 megabyte
Gigabyte (GB)	1024 megabytes = 1 gigabyte
Terabyte (TB)	1024 gigabytes = 1 terabyte

In the context of data and information in computers, data is stored in the form of bits and bytes, whereas information could be time, data, folder name, etc.

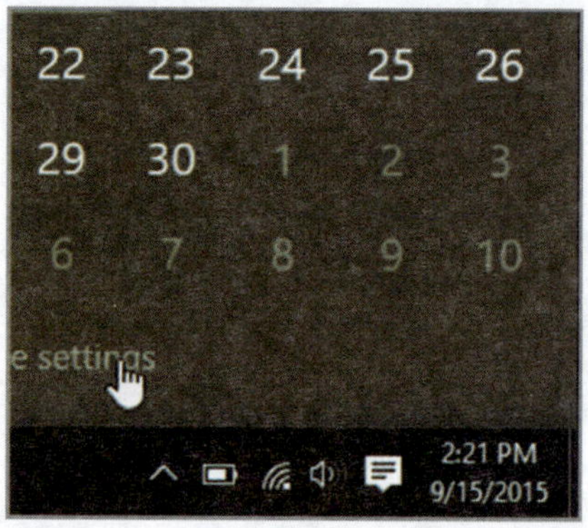

Fig. 1.1 | *Time and Date displayed on Windows 10*

Computer Memory

Memory represents the total available storage space in a computer. Memory cannot accommodate a file whose size exceeds its capacity. For example, a 1.2 GB movie cannot be stored in a disk whose size is 1 GB.

Internal Memory

Internal memory in a computer is the memory that is directly accessible by the processor. It is also called the primary or main memory of the computer. RAM and ROM are the two types of internal memory.

Clear up!

Navigate to your favourite image or song file on your computer. Right-click on the file and then select **Properties**. Did you find the size of the file?

Random Access Memory (RAM)

Random Access Memory can be accessed directly by the CPU. It is the read/write memory. Information can be read from and written onto RAM. It stores the data that the user is using while working on the computer. If the computer is switched off, the data in its memory will be lost. RAM is, therefore, referred to as volatile memory.

Read Only Memory (ROM)

Read Only Memory is the computer memory from which information can only be read. Information cannot be written or erased from ROM. This memory is a non-volatile memory.

External Memory

The external memory of a computer refers to permanent storage devices. It is also known as auxiliary storage, secondary memory or flash memory. Secondary memory is non-volatile, which means that data does not get deleted even when the device is powered off. The data remains intact till it is deleted or overwritten. Following are the examples of secondary memory.

auxiliary storage: extra storage that is available for use when necessary

- **Optical Discs**: An optical disc is a rotating disc made of material like aluminium, which is used to store and read data. Optical discs use low-power laser light to write data onto a disc. Compact Discs (CDs), Digital Video Discs (DVDs) and Blu-ray discs are variations of optical discs. A CD can hold 650–700 MB data. A DVD can hold 4.7–8.7 GB data while a Blu-ray disc can hold 25–50 GB data.

Fig. 1.2 | *DVD in a DVD player*

- **Hard Disk Drive (HDD)**: Hard drives or hard disks are used to store large amount of data. There are two types of hard disks: (i) internal (Fig. 1.3) and (ii) external (Fig. 1.4). The Internal Hard Disk Drive is found inside the CPU, which serves as the storage mechanism for the computer. External Hard Disk Drives are portable and can be plugged into a laptop or a personal computer using a cable. Their storage capacity ranges from 3.75 MB to 16 TB (as of 2020).

Fig. 1.3 | *Internal hard drive*

Fig. 1.4 | *External hard drive*

- **USB drive**: USB stands for **universal serial bus** (Fig. 1.5). The USB port in a CPU is an opening (port) that allows devices or cables to be plugged in. The USB drive is a portable drive that can be plugged into the CPU. It allows high-speed transfer of data to and from the computers. They are also known as **flash drives or pen drives**. The storage capacity of USB drives is up to 2 TB.

Fig. 1.5 | *USB drive plugged into the USB port*

- **Solid State Drives (SSDs)**: These drives are also known as SD cards (Fig. 1.6). Solid state drives are thin cards that can be plugged into a computer or a laptop. The maximum storage capacity of SD cards is 128 TB currently.

SD cards and USB drives use **flash memory**. Flash memory is made up of flash memory cells, which are electronic circuits that store one bit of binary information (1: on, 0: off). Data can be electronically written and erased from flash drives. In other words, SD cards and USB devices are electronic, non-volatile storage media that can be electrically erased and reprogrammed.

Fig. 1.6 | *SD card*

Link up!

Micro SD cards are used in smartphones as external storage. Most smartphones have a provision to plug in the micro SD card or have a tray on which the micro SD card can be placed and inserted into the device.

Soak up!

Due to the advancement in data storage capabilities, it is now possible to store and process large amounts of data on computers. When the numbers are big and the relationship between things is complex, it is important to represent them accurately, yet effectively.

Data visualization is the use of graphics to represent data. It uses shapes, charts, text, colours and other visual elements. Data visualization can be static pictures or interactive presentations. Here are some of examples of how data visualization helps us make sense of the data.

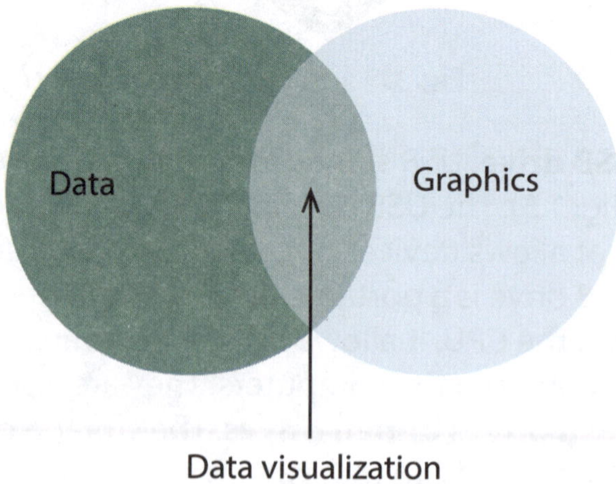

Emerging Disciplines in Data

Data is becoming increasingly valuable nowadays because of two reasons:

1. The internet has enabled a large number of people to interact online, either to access information or to buy and sell products.
2. Large amounts of data, collected from various sources, can be effectively stored because of the advancements in storage technology and related applications.

However, a collection of raw data will not provide any meaningful insights unless it is analysed properly. This is where the term **data analysis** comes into the picture.

Data analytics and related fields, such as data mining, data warehousing and data science, are fast-evolving fields of study.

> Data analytics is the examination of raw data in order to gather insights from it.

Big Data

Many fields, such as medicine, transportation, banking, education and manufacturing are being increasingly fueled by technology. This results in huge amounts of data being generated by the end-users and also the system processes, thus making it complex. Data is generated in the range of petabytes or higher (1 petabyte = 1,000 terabytes).

> Big data refers to large amounts of structured and unstructured data that grows with time. It cannot be processed with the help of traditional techniques and requires special tools.

Today I learned!

- Data is a collection of facts, concepts or instructions.
- Information is processed data on which decisions and actions are based.
- Computer memory is of two kinds: primary and secondary.
- Primary memory can be of two kinds: RAM and ROM.
- RAM is volatile memory. Information stored in RAM is lost when the computer is switched off.
- ROM is non-volatile memory. Information stored in ROM is not lost if the computer is switched off.
- Secondary memory refers to storage devices, such as hard disks and pen drives, which can be connected to a computer. It can be used to store information permanently.
- Examples of secondary memory include Compact Disc (CD), Hard Disk Drive (HDD), universal serial bus (USB) drive and Solid State Drives (SSDs).

Revise and polish!

Learning Skills

1. Tick (✔) the correct answer.

a. Which of the following storage devices uses flash memory?

(i) SD cards ☐ (ii) RAM ☐ (iii) ROM ☐ (iv) Volatile ☐

b. Which of the following is the fastest way to access data in the primary memory?

(i) RAM ☐ (ii) ROM ☐

(iii) Hard disk ☐ (iv) Cables ☐

c. In which of the following types of storage devices is data saved temporarily?

(i) USB drive ☐ (ii) Compact disk ☐

(iii) RAM ☐ (iv) Cloud ☐

d. Which of the following are variations of optical disks?

(i) DVD ☐ (ii) CD ☐

(iii) All of the above ☐ (iv) Pen drive ☐

e. Eight bits make one ___________.

(i) GB ☐ (ii) MB ☐ (iii) byte ☐ (iv) TB ☐

2. Fill in the blanks using the given words.

eight primary non-volatile data information

a. Data and ___________ are important in computing.

b. ___________ bits form a byte.

c. Internal memory is also known as ___________ memory.

d. Secondary memory is ___________.

e. Big data refers to large amounts of structured and unstructured ___________.

3. Match the following.

a.	Information	(i)	1024 megabytes
b.	Memory	(ii)	1024 gigabytes
c.	1 GB	(iii)	Data + Meaning
d.	1 TB	(iv)	1024 kilobytes
e.	1 MB	(v)	Total space in a computer

4. Look at the given data. Then, read each of the clues. Follow them to complete the information.

Data:

A B C D E F G H I J K L M N O P Q R S T U V W X Y Z

Information

a. Name of animals (three-letter words only) ______________________

b. Name of things (four-letter words only) ______________________

c. Name of places (five-letter words only)______________________

d. Name of subjects (seven-letter words only) ______________________

Congratulations! You have just converted data into information.

5. **Differentiate between the following.**

a. RAM and ROM
b. Internal memory and external memory
c. Data and information

6. **Answer the following questions.**

a. What do you understand by a bit?
b. Give the full form of CD and DVD.
c. What is flash memory?
d. Write a short note on USB drives.
e. Explain big data.

Lab Activity

Experiential Learning

1. In the lab, discuss the following questions with your computer teacher.
   a. How to check the RAM size of your computer?
   b. What was invented first among the CDs, DVDs and Blu-ray discs?
   c. In which year was the first pen drive launched?
2. Collect pictures of all external storage devices in your computer. Make a list of all these devices using MS Word.
3. Using the internet in the computer lab, find out if and how data can be stored on the web.

Think and Answer

Problem-solving | Critical thinking

Name the storage mechanism/devices used for the following purposes:

1. Radha has downloaded some insightful videos from the internet for her project on glaciers. They are 1.5 GB in size. Which external storage device(s) can she use to give the video to her project team member?

   ____

2. Roshan played a racing game on his computer. He closed the application and switched OFF the computer after some time. In which memory was the game loaded while it was in use?

   ____

3. Arjun's grandmother purchased a new smartphone. She wants to listen to old songs on her smartphone that can be accessed even without the internet or on YouTube. Which storage device can Arjun use to load the songs onto the smartphone to help his grandmother?

   ____

Chapter 2

GUI Operating System—Desktop Management

After reading this chapter, I will be able to:

- ✔ Recall the features of OS and GUI.
- ✔ Identify and use the Taskbar, Quick launch bar and the shortcut menu.
- ✔ Customize the Windows setup.

Technology Literacy

Brainstorm and explore!

Look at this picture. Can you guess what it shows? Write your answer in the space below.

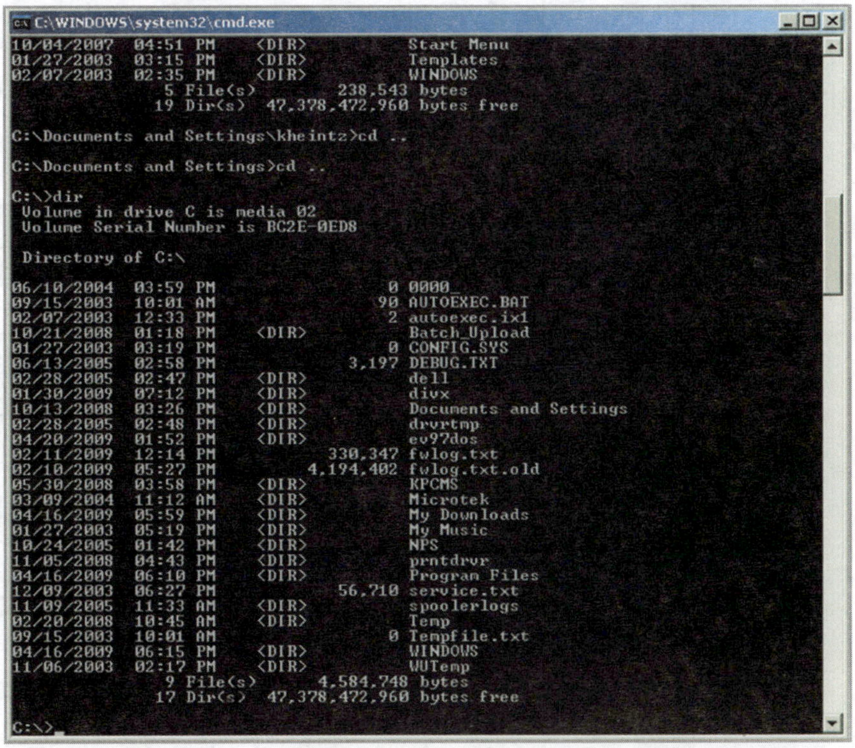

____

____

____

____

____

____

____

____

The figure that you saw on the previous page is an example of a **command line interface (CLI)-based operating system**. The earliest computers were not powerful enough to be able to use visuals or pictures. The only way we could interact with such computers was by typing instructions. Thus, the interface was based on command lines. In a CLI-based operating system, commands were used to give input, and the output was received in the textual format.

We have learned about graphical user interface-based operating systems in the previous class. In a GUI-based operating system, icons and graphics are used to interact with the computer.

Clear up!

Recall the meaning of desktop from the previous class and discuss with your classmates.

Operating System

We know that an operating system (OS) connects the computer hardware with software used in the computer and vice-versa. It makes sure that all programs on the computer (software) have access to the keyboard, mouse, CPU and other devices (hardware). An OS helps us run the entire computer.

As shown in Fig. 2.1, users give instructions to various software programs. These instructions are then given to the OS that further passes instructions to the hardware. For example, if we give the Print command to MS Paint program, the OS sends instructions to the printer to print the pictures.

Soak up!

The process of the operating system loading when a computer is turned on is called booting.

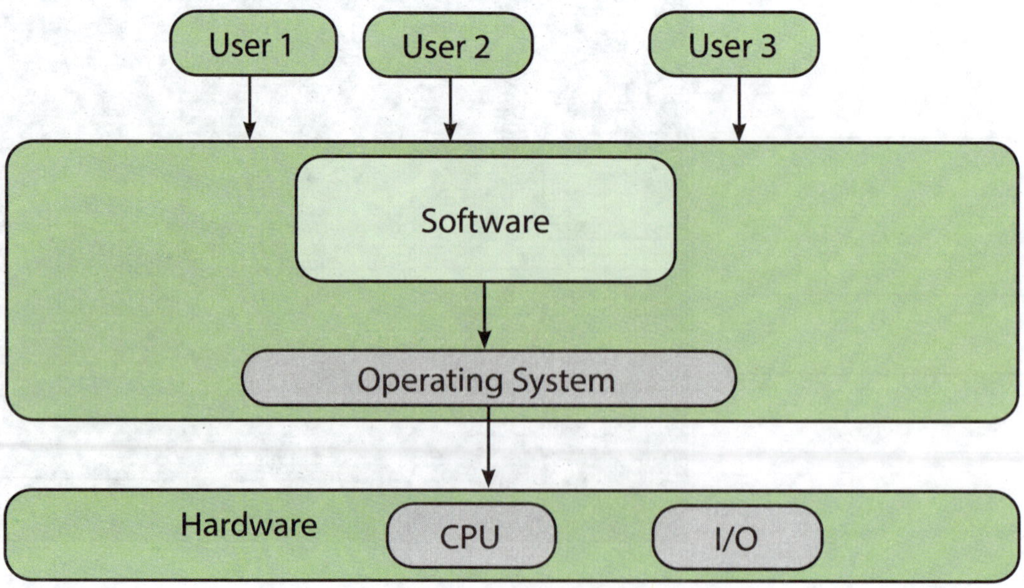

Fig. 2.1 | *Working of an operating system*

Windows 10

Windows 10 is an operating system launched by Microsoft in the year 2015.

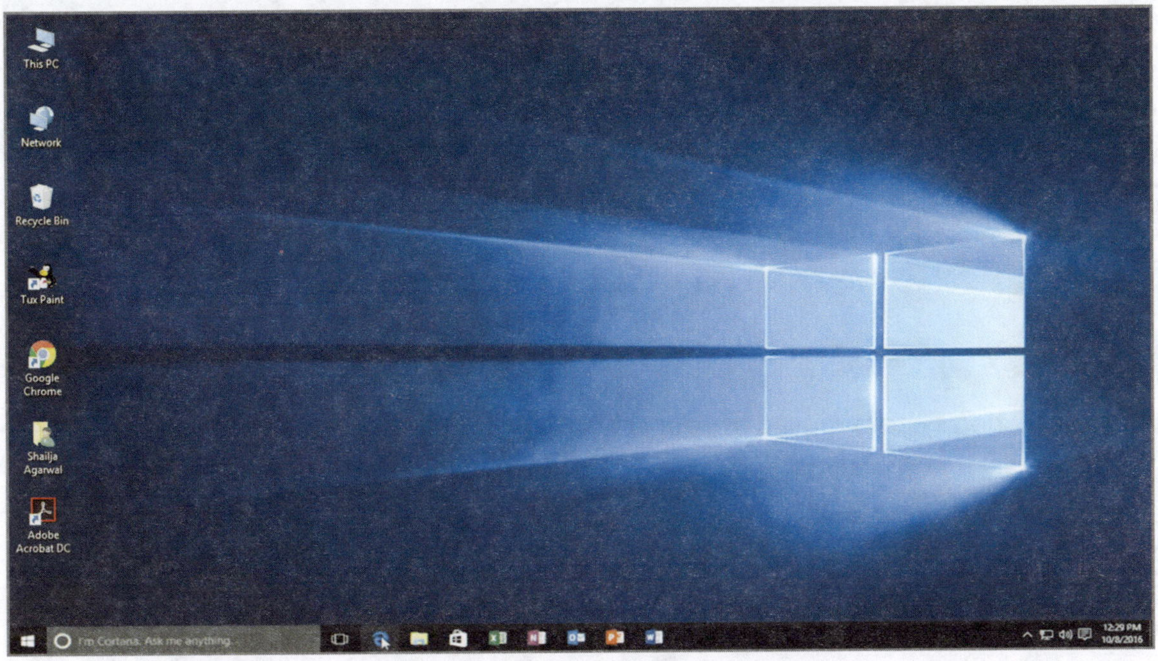

Fig. 2.2 | *Desktop of Windows 10 OS*

> **Link up!**
>
> Developments in technology have made it accessible to more and more people. For example, as computers became more powerful, they also became smaller and cheaper. Further the introduction to GUI has made it easy-to-use computers. There was no need to learn a specialized computer language.

Windows has a ***Graphical User Interface (GUI)***, as shown in Fig. 2.2. This means that it uses picture-like items (the mouse pointer/icons used for folders). Different icons are used for different file types. This makes it the most commonly used operating system. Some of its advantages are given below:

> **Soak up!**
>
> Microsoft was founded by Bill Gates and Paul Allen. As of 2022, Satya Nadella, who is of Indian origin, is the CEO of this corporation.

1. It is very easy to use.
2. It works with most software programs.
3. There are many applications and games available for download on the Windows OS.
4. It is the most widely used OS for desktop computers in the world.

icon: a picture that helps us identify programs on a computer

Technology Literacy

Crank up!

The computers in school labs have Windows 7, Windows 8 or Windows 10, that is, versions of Windows OS. We can find out the OS version by right-clicking on the **This PC** icon, then selecting **Properties**.

Brush up!

1. Which operating system is used in your school computer lab?

   ____

2. Write the name of five programs installed on the computers.

   ____

   ____

Components of Windows 10 Desktop

Windows 10 is a user-friendly operating system. It contains different components as shown in Fig. 2.3.

Fig. 2.3 | *Components of Windows 10 desktop*

Start button: The Start button is placed on the bottom-left corner of the screen. It is used to access and view all applications on the computer. The applications are usually listed with their names and icons under the Start menu (Fig. 2.4). We can access the Start menu either by left-clicking on the Windows icon or by pressing the windows key on the keyboard.

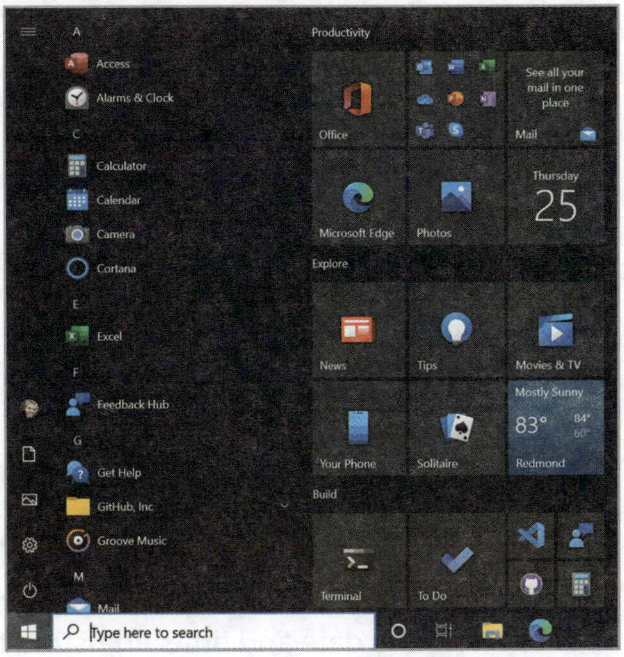

Fig. 2.4 | *Start menu*

Taskbar: The taskbar is usually placed at the bottom of the desktop. It enables the user to manage and navigate different applications, connect with the Internet, etc.

Search bar: The Search bar is present on the left side of the Taskbar. It enables text and voice search of files and folders on the computer. The search bar is also known as the **Cortana bar**.

Soak up!

Cortana is a virtual assistant created by Microsoft to help answer the user's questions. This is similar to Siri of MacOS and iOS.

Quick launch bar: This bar enables users to quickly open applications that are frequently used, such as Microsoft Edge, Microsoft Office, Notepad and so on. This bar is found at the bottom of the screen, next to Cortana (Fig. 2.5).

Fig. 2.5 | *Quick launch bar*

Notification area: This appears at the bottom right corner of the screen (Fig. 2.6). The Notification area is used to display an array of information including the following options:

- Date and time
- Wi-Fi shortcut
- Sound status
- Battery status and much more

Fig. 2.6 | *Notification area*

A limited number of icons can be shown on the Notification area. To see more icons, users need to click on the upward arrow (^).

Soak up!

A USB drive is a portable storage device used to store files and folders. It can be plugged into a computer for use. When a USB drive is inserted in a computer or laptop the USB icon is displayed in the Notification area. It is advisable to right-click on the USB icon and select the **Eject External USB 3.0**  option before removing the device.

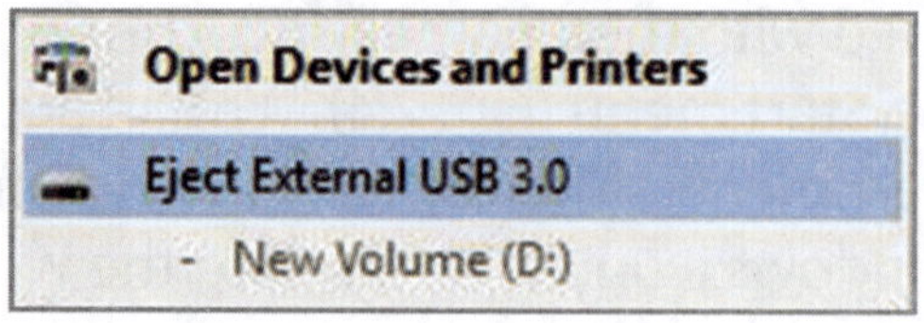

Changing Settings on Windows 10

Many features of Windows 10 can be customized to match user preferences. Let us learn about setting the date and time, adjusting the volume of speaker and changing the position of the Taskbar.

Setting Date and Time

The date and time on Windows operating system can be changed. They can be changed together or even separately. The steps to change date and time are as follows:

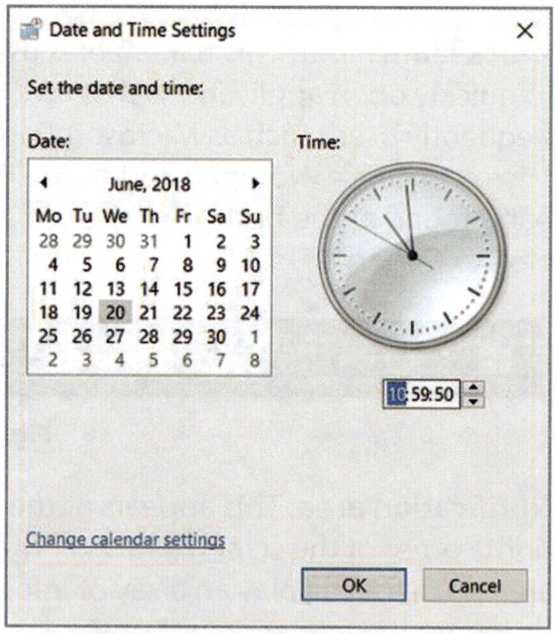

Fig. 2.7 | *Date and Time Settings dialog box*

1. Click on the **Start button** → **Windows System** → **Control Panel** or type 'Control Panel' in the Search bar. Click on the **Control Panel** icon to open it.
2. Click on **Clock and Region** → **Date and Time**. The **Date and Time** dialog box opens (Fig. 2.7).
3. Click on the **Change date and time** button. The **Date and Time Settings** dialog box appears and displays a calendar and a clock.
   (i) To change the date, select the required date on the calendar. The ◀ and ▶ arrows can be used to navigate among months.
   (ii) To change the time, use the ▲ and ▼ arrows to change the hours, minutes and seconds.
4. After setting the date and time, click on the **OK** button.

Setting Volume of the Speaker

Click on the **Speaker** icon in the **Notification area** (Fig. 2.8). Use the mouse to click on the volume level and drag it to adjust to the desired volume.

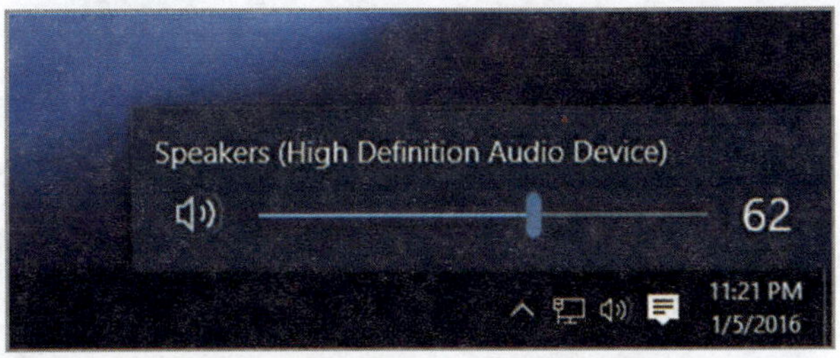

Fig. 2.8 | *Volume icon in the Notification area*

Changing the Position of the Taskbar

It is not mandatory for the taskbar to be on the bottom of the screen! The position of the taskbar can be changed to the left, right and top of the screen as well.

The steps for the same are as follows:

1. Right-click on the taskbar on an empty place and click on the **Taskbar settings** option (Fig. 2.9). This opens a window to customize the taskbar.

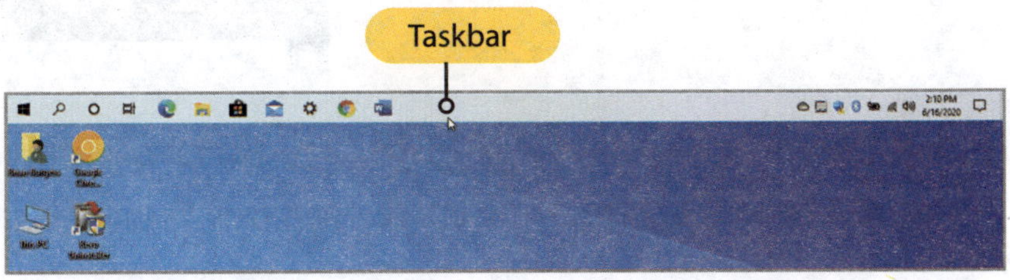

Fig. 2.9 | *Taskbar at the top of the screen*

2. Scroll down to **Taskbar** at the right pane on screen.
3. In the left pane, click on the drop-down options under the **Taskbar location on screen** and select the desired position of the taskbar.

Use of the Shortcut Menu

Upon right-clicking any icon or on the desktop, a menu appears that has several options for actions associated with the icon or the desktop. Figure 2.10 depicts the options available when we click on the blank area on the desktop. Figure 2.11 depicts the options available when we click on an icon on the desktop.

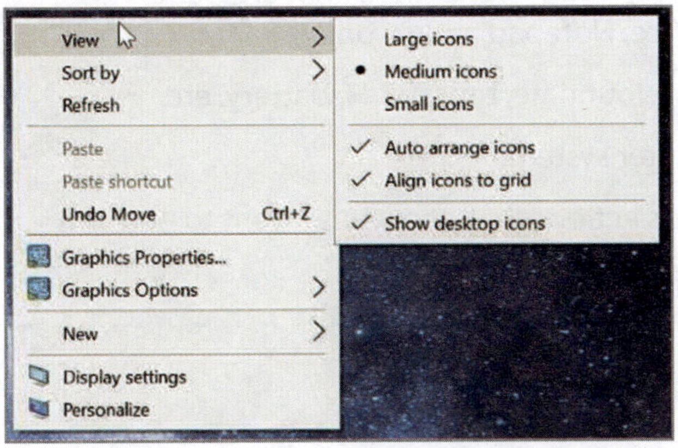

Fig. 2.10 | *Right-clicking on the desktop*

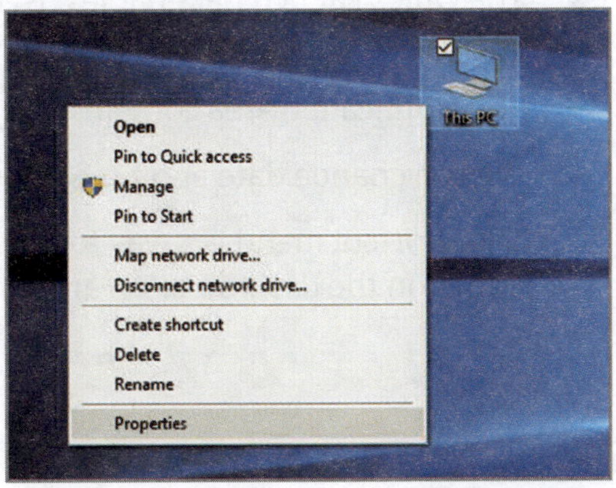

Fig. 2.11 | *Right-clicking on This PC icon*

Fun with AI

Cortana is the Window's virtual, digital assistant. It also enables search through voice recognition. To identify speech and process it, Artificial Intelligence is used. Voice Recognition and Natural Language Processing algorithms are used for the same.

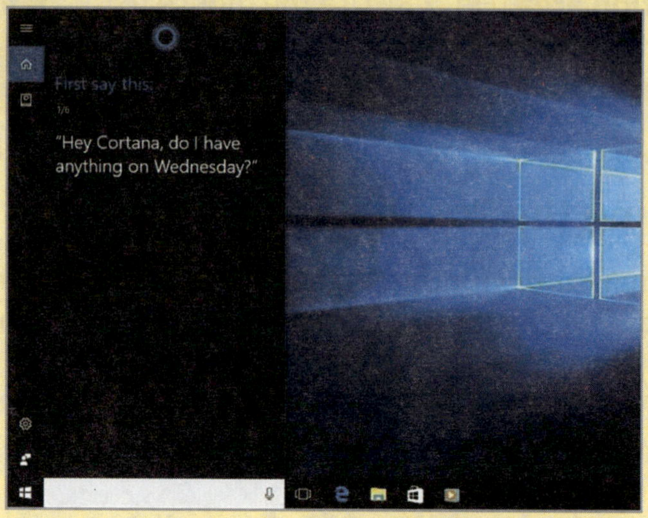

Today I learned!

- Windows is a Graphical User Interface (GUI)-based operating system. It uses icons instead of commands.
- An icon is a picture that helps us identify a program on the computer screen.
- Windows 10 is a user-friendly operating system.
- The Start button is used to access and view all the applications on the computer.
- The Taskbar is the band on Windows desktop that enables the user to manage and navigate different applications, connect with the internet, search files, etc.
- Cortana enables text and voice search of files and folders on the computer.
- The Quick Launch bar enables users to quickly open applications that are frequently used, such as Microsoft Edge, Microsoft Office, Notepad and so on.
- The Notification area contains information about date, time, Wi-Fi, battery, etc.
- We can change date and time of our computer system.
- The shortcut menu is a way to quickly access actions that one would want to perform either on the desktop or on an icon on the desktop.

Revise and polish!

Learning Skills

1. Tick (✓) the correct answer.

a. Which of the following is a way to quickly access actions that we would want to perform either on the desktop or on an icon on the desktop?

(i) Start menu ☐ (ii) Recycle Bin ☐

(iii) Shortcut menu ☐ (iv) Control Panel ☐

b. Which of the following contains information about date, time, Wi-Fi, battery, etc.?

(i) Desktop ☐ (ii) Search bar ☐

(iii) Notification area ☐ (iv) Cortana ☐

c. Which of the following is the band on Windows desktop that enables users to manage and navigate different applications, connect the Internet, search files, etc.?

(i) Shortcut menu ☐ (ii) URL ☐

(iii) Taskbar ☐ (iv) Browser ☐

d. In which year was Windows 10 launched?

(i) 2015 ☐ (ii) 2016 ☐

(iii) 2017 ☐ (iv) 2019 ☐

e. Which of the following is not a part of the taskbar?

(i) Start button ☐ (ii) Recycle Bin ☐

(iii) Quick launch bar ☐ (iv) My Computer ☐

2. Fill in the blanks using the given words.

Windows 11 icon operating system Search command line interface

a. CLI stands for ______________.

b. An ______________ is a picture that helps us identify a program on the computer screen.

c. The latest version of Windows OS is ______________.

d. The ______________ connects the hardware with software.

e. The ______________ bar is also known as the Cortana bar.

3. Match the following.

a.	Start button	(i)	Helps manage and navigate applications
b.	Taskbar	(ii)	Also called Cortana bar
c.	Search bar	(iii)	Displays an array of information
d.	Notification area	(iv)	Opens frequently used applications
e.	Quick launch bar	(v)	Displays the Start menu

4. State whether the following statements are true (T) or false (F).

a. An operating system (OS) connects the computer hardware to software used in the computer. ☐

b. Windows 10 was launched by IBM in 2010. ☐

c. Different icons are used for different file types. ☐

d. We cannot access the Start button in GUI. ☐

e. The search bar is also known as the Cortana bar. ☐

5. Answer the following questions.

a. Write a short note on GUI.

b. Where is the Taskbar present on the desktop? Give the steps to change its position.

c. Give the uses of the Start button.

d. What is Cortana?

e. What is the Quick launch bar?

Lab Activities

Experiential Learning

1. List the different icons present on the desktop of your computer. Sort these icons alphabetically.

2. Open MS Paint using the Search bar. Pin this program on the Taskbar of your computer.

Think and Answer

Problem-solving | Critical thinking

1. You have bought a new computer and the date shows as 20/12/2011. How will you reset the date to the current date?

____

____

2. You are working on a project and need to access the browser frequently. What can you do to make the browser easily accessible?

____

____

3. You are listening to music on your computer. The volume of the speaker is very loud, and your sibling is complaining about the noise. How will you adjust the volume?

____

____

Project

Collaboration

Along with a classmate, create a desktop of the future. Include any applications or features that you think will enhance the utility and look-and-feel of the desktop. Draw and colour the desktop of the future on a chart paper and present it to the class. Remember there are no limits to your imagination!

Chapter 3

Tools of Word Processor

After reading this chapter, I will be able to:

- ✔ Edit and format a document in MS Word.
- ✔ Demonstrate the use of Spelling and Grammar check.
- ✔ Describe the use of Thesaurus.
- ✔ Change the font style, color and type.
- ✔ Demonstrate the use of line spacing, paragraph spacing and shortcut keys.
- ✔ Print a document and use print preview.

Brainstorm and explore!

If you are writing a sentence using a pencil and want to change the sentence or correct a mistake, which tool would you use from the pencil box? Give the steps for correcting a mistake on paper.

____

____

____

____

____

An eraser is used to correct mistakes or make changes while writing. In MS Word, modifications can be made to a document even after creating the document or a part of it. This is known as **editing a document**.

Editing is the process of making changes to a document.

Using Undo and Redo Commands

In previous classes, we have learned about adding text to a document and using the Cut, Copy and Paste options. Two more options are used to edit documents effectively.

The Undo and Redo buttons are available on the Quick Access Toolbar (Fig. 3.1). The Undo button is used to cancel the last action performed. The Redo button is used to reverse the actions of the Undo button.

Fig. 3.1 | *Undo and Redo buttons*

The keyboard shortcut Ctrl+X can also be used to Undo an action. The keyboard shortcut for the Redo an action is Ctrl+Y or F4.

Link up!

Books and magazines have professional editors who ensure the published material is relevant, accurate and interesting!

Checking Spelling and Grammar

MS Word is used for typing letters, documents, reports, etc. If a spelling is typed incorrectly, the automatic spell checker of MS Word application points it out by underlining the incorrect word with a red, wavy line. MS Word has an inbuilt dictionary, using which it constantly checks for incorrect spellings and grammatical error in the text, thus making them easy to locate and correct.

To see the suggested corrections, right-click on the underlined word and click on the correct spelling to replace the incorrect one (Fig. 3.2).

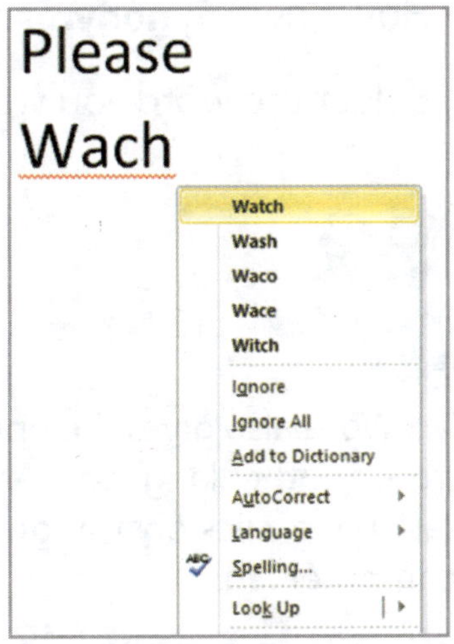

Fig. 3.2 | *Right-clicking on the word to see suggestions*

We can also look for the errors using the Preview Pane that appears upon clicking the spell check icon in the status bar, at the bottom left of the screen. This pane appears on the right side of the screen and shows all the incorrect spellings the computer finds in the document. It also provides the following options:

- **Ignore Once**: This option tells the software to skip the error one time.
- **Ignore All**: This option tells the software that all the occurrence of the word is to be considered correct throughout the document.
- **Add to Dictionary**: This option tells the software to add the word to dictionary, so that it is not considered wrong, even if we start working on a new document.

Alternatively, select abc Check Document button from the **Proofing** group of the **Review** tab to check spelling and grammar in MS Word 2016.

Thesaurus

Do you know what synonyms are? Could you write the synonyms for the following words?

Small: ____________ Tidy: ____________ Quick: ____________

These are simple words, and synonyms can be recollected quickly. While composing a sentence, the use of one word might be more appropriate than its synonym.

✗ The cat moved promptly

✓ The cat moved swiftly

The Thesaurus feature in MS Word allows us to use the synonyms for any word. Following are the steps to use this feature.

1. Select the word that you want to find the synonym for.
2. Right-click on the word and navigate to synonym.
3. Hover over **Synonyms** and it will show the list of synonyms.
4. Select the word you want to use.

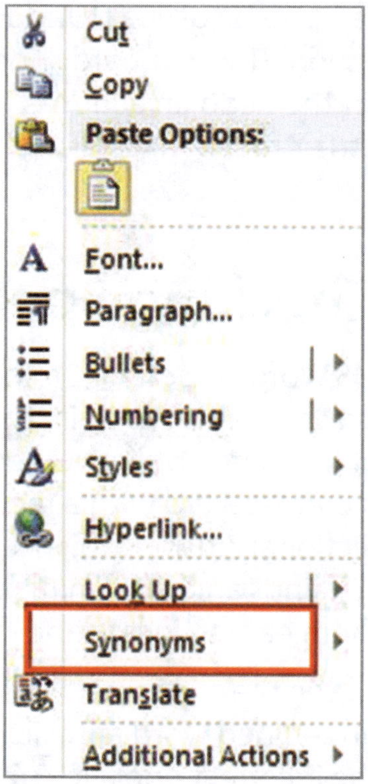

Fig. 3.3 | *Using* Thesaurus to find *synonyms of a word*

Technology Literacy

Crank up!

MS Word also gives the option of selecting the word from another language. At the bottom of the Thesaurus task pane, click on a language. Explore this option in the computer lab.

Line Alignment

MS Word allows us to determine the alignment of the text we type in a document. There are three alignment options available to us:

1. **Align Left**: This option makes the text shift towards the left margin of the document. This is the default option in MS Word.
2. **Center**: This option makes the text shift towards the centre, between the left and the right margin.
3. **Align Right**: This option makes the text shift towards the right margin of the document.

Line Spacing and Paragraph Spacing

Could you identify the formatting difference between the texts in the boxes below?

"The quick brown fox jumps over the lazy dog" is an English-language pangram—a sentence that contains all of the letters of the English alphabet. Owing to its brevity and coherence, it has become widely known.

Source: Wikipedia

'The quick brown fox jumps over the lazy dog' is an English-language pangram—a sentence that contains all of the letters of the English alphabet. Owing to its brevity and coherence, it has become widely known.

Source: Wikipedia

The space between the lines is different, and this is referred to as **Line Spacing**. Following are the steps to use the line spacing option in MS Word:

1. Select the text to be formatted.
2. Under the **Home** tab, click on the **Line and Paragraph** spacing button (Fig. 3.4).
3. From the options, select the desired spacing.

The space between paragraphs is known as **paragraph spacing**. The steps to apply paragraph spacing are similar to those for line spacing, except there are only two options to increase or decrease the space between paragraphs.

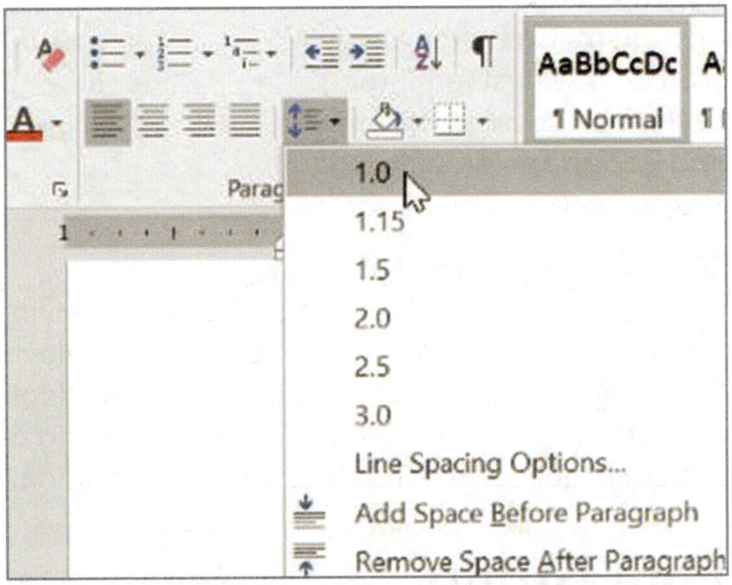

Fig. 3.4 | *Line and Paragraph spacing*

Brush up!

In the computer lab, type the text in the above example. Apply all different kinds of line spacing and observe the difference.

Fun with AI

Artificial Intelligence is used to identify grammatical errors in sentences and provide suggestions for correction. Grammarly is one such tool that can be used on the browser.

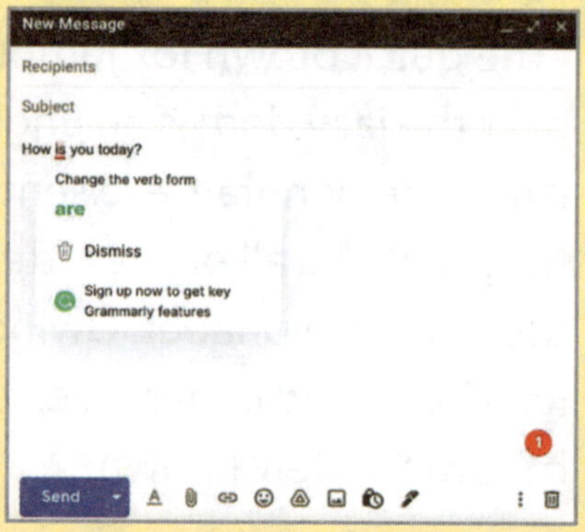

Formatting a Document

Formatting helps us bring out the important information in our document and to organize a document in a better way. In MS Word 2016, most formatting options are located in the **Font** and **Paragraph** groups under the **Home** tab (Fig. 3.5).

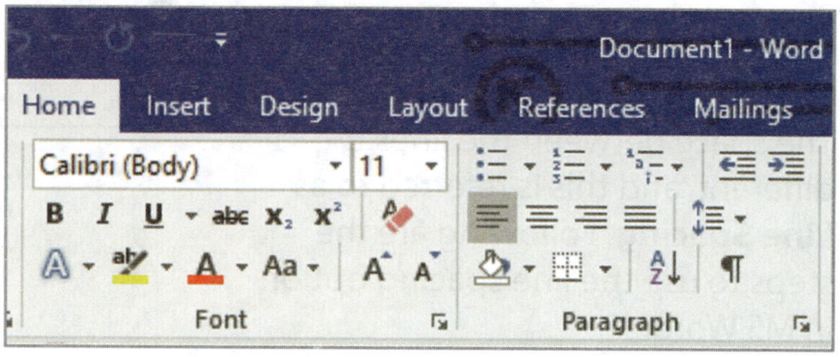

Fig. 3.5 | *Font and Paragraph group*

Editing is the process of making changes to the document, which include removing or modifying the text, moving it and making it relevant. Formatting, on the other hand, deals with the look and appearance of the text in the document. Editing deals with structure, and formatting deals with presentation.

Modifying the appearance of text is known as formatting.

Font Group

In MS Word, there are many options for adjusting the font of the text including type, size and colours. Let us learn about these in detail.

Changing the Font of Text

We can change the style of the text by changing its font. The steps to change the text font are given below:

1. Select the text for which the font needs to be changed.

2. Click on the drop-down arrow next to the **Font** in the **Font** group.
3. Scroll through the list of fonts in the **Font drop-down** menu that appears (Fig. 3.6). Notice that the names of fonts are written differently. This is because each font name is also a preview of how the text will look when you choose that font.
4. Click on the desired font.

The font will be changed for the selected text in the document.

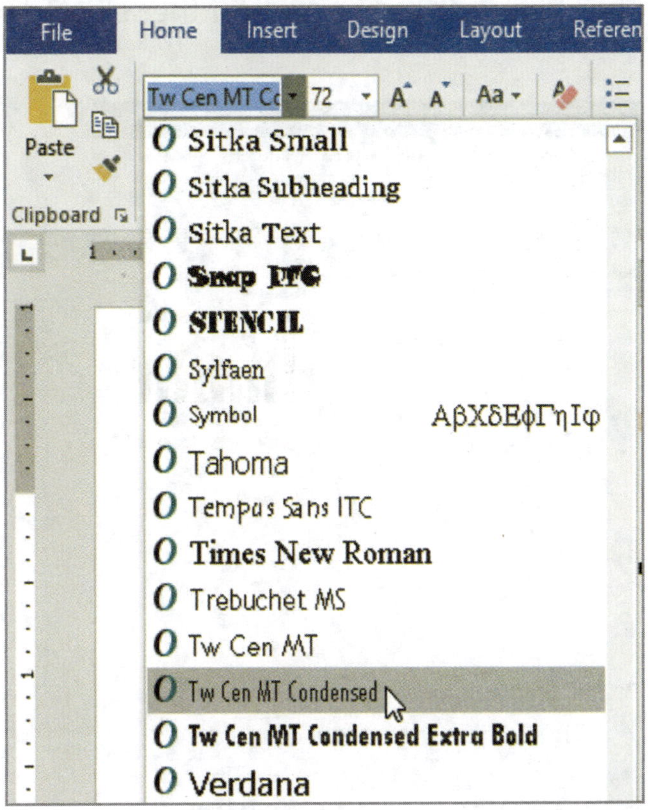

Fig. 3.6 | *Font drop-down menu*

Soak up!

Default settings are the settings that are applied unless a change is made. The default font in MS Word is Calibri (Body).

Crank up! Technology Literacy

The size of the text can also be changed the same way we change the font. Try it out and see the results for various sizes.

The size of the text in a document can also be changed using the button given aside the Font button.

The **Increase Font Size** and **Decrease Font Size** commands in the **Font** group under the **Home** tab can also be used to change the font size.

Font Color

The default colour of text in MS Word is black. The steps to change the font colour are given below:

1. Select the text for which the colour needs to be changed.
2. Click on the **Font Color** drop-down arrow under the **Home** tab.
3. Select the desired font colour from the various options in the **Font Color drop-down** menu that appears.

The colour will be changed for the selected text in the document (Fig. 3.7).

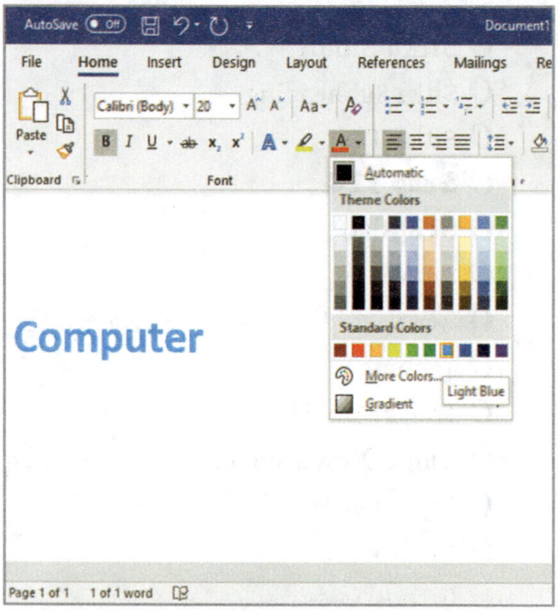

Fig. 3.7 | *Changing font colour of text*

Technology Literacy

Crank up!

Highlighting the text means marking it with a colour in the background of the text. The text can be highlighted using the **Text Highlight Color** option in the **Font** group under the **Home** tab.

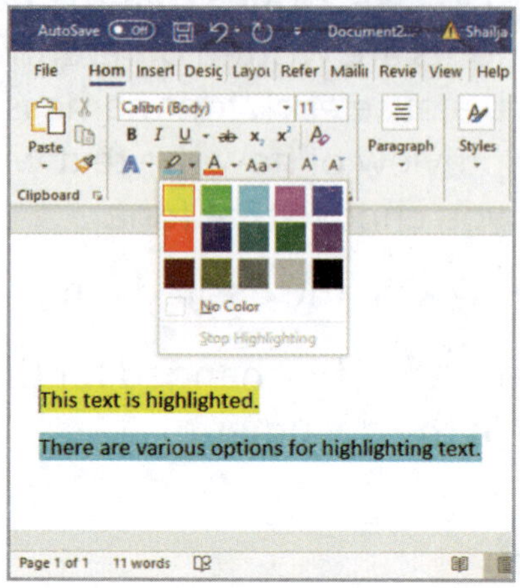

Bold, Italic and Underline

We can emphasize the text by making it **bold**, *italic* or by <u>underlining</u> it. For applying any of these styles, select the text to be modified and then select the **Bold** B , **Italic** I or **Underline** U button from the **Font** group (Fig. 3.8).

Note that you can select more than one option at the same time—you can make the desired text bold, underlined and italicized.

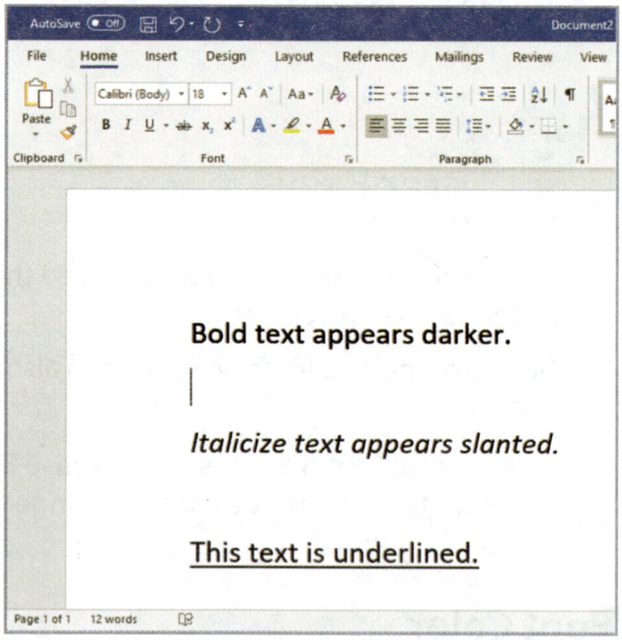

Fig. 3.8 | *Making text Bold, Italic and Underline*

Changing Case of the Text

We have learned about capital and small letters while learning letters. The steps to change text case are given below:

1. Select the text for which the case needs to be changed.
2. Click on the **Change Case** button in the **Font** group under the **Home** tab and then select the desired option from the list (Fig. 3.9). The various common forms of writing sentences in MS Word are:

   Sentence case: The first letter of the first word of the sentence is capitalized.

lowercase: All the characters are in lowercase (small letters).

UPPERCASE: All the characters are in uppercase (capital letters).

Capitalize Each Word: The first letter of each word is capitalized.

tOGGLE cASE: The uppercase and lowercase letters are interchanged.

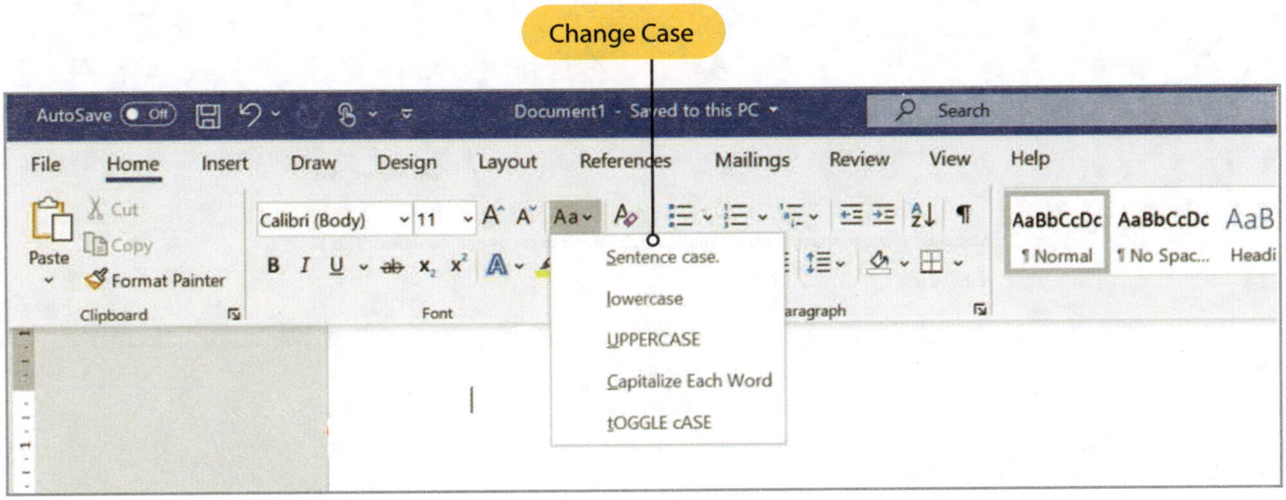

Fig. 3.9 | *Change Case drop down menu*

Paragraph Group

The **Paragraph** group under the **Home** tab has many options to fine-tune the layout of the current paragraph, including spacing, alignment and more. Let us learn about these in detail.

Aligning the Text

Alignment refers to where the text is placed with respect to the overall document.

We can change the text alignment by following these steps:

1. Select the text for which the alignment needs to be changed.
2. In the **Paragraph** group under the **Home** tab, there are four **text alignment** options to choose from (Fig. 3.10):

   Align Left ≡ : Aligns all text to the left margin.

   Center ≡ : Aligns text at an equal distance from the left and the right margins.

   Align Right ≡ : Aligns all text to the right margin.

   Justify ≡ : Aligns text equally along both margins.

After selecting the desired option, the text will be aligned.

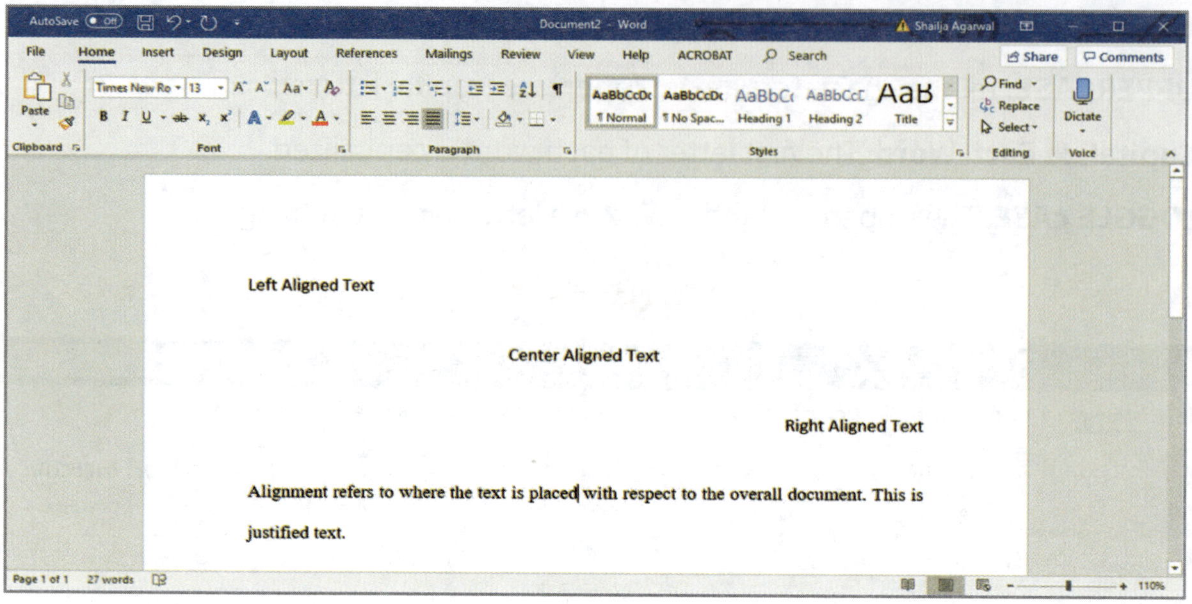

Fig. 3.10 | *Text alignment*

Preview and Printing

MS Word also gives us the option to print the document once we are finished with creating, editing and formatting it. It also gives us the option to see how the document would look on a page. This is called the **Preview** feature (Fig. 3.11).

We can preview the document by following the steps given below:

1. Click on the **File** tab.
2. Select the **Print** option.

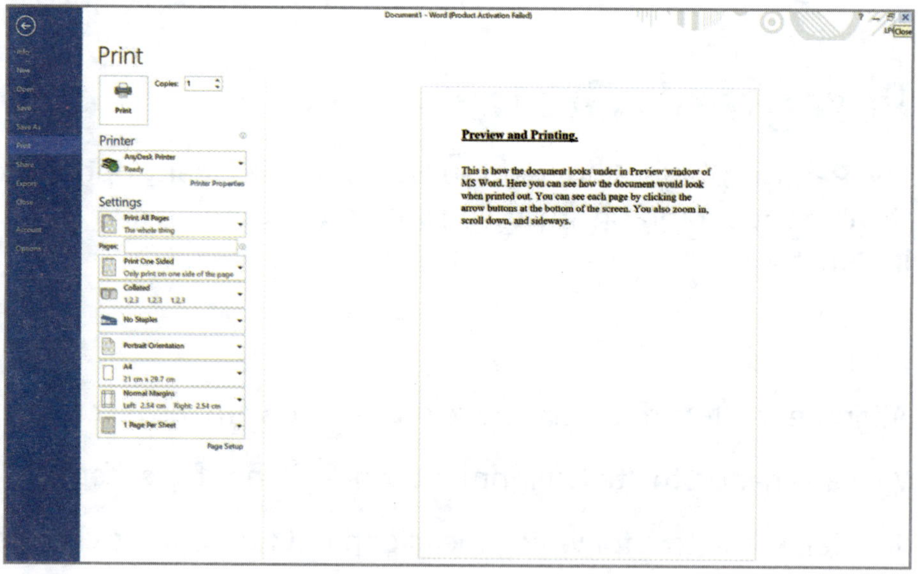

Fig. 3.11 | *The Preview Window*

The Preview window provides us with much information, such as how each page would look when printed out, and a magnifying glass symbol which zooms in on the document.

Printing the Document

After previewing the document, we are now ready to print it out. Do this by selecting the printer from the drop-down menu under the Printer option. We can also choose the number of copies to be made. Besides, MS Word also gives us the option to select the pages that we want to print out. These are as follows:

1. The **Print All** option prints out all the pages in a document.
2. The **Print Selection** prints out all the selected text in a document.
3. The **Print Current Page** only prints out the current page.
4. The **Custom Print** helps us specify a range that we want to print out.

We can now print out the document by clicking on the **Print** button.

Technology Literacy

Crank up!

Shortcut keys are a way to save time and work on MS Word (or any application) in a faster, smarter manner.

Some important keyboard shortcuts in MS Word 2016 are given below:

Action	Keyboard Shortcut
Bold	Ctrl+B
Italic	Ctrl+I
Underline	Ctrl+U
Switch between different cases (after selecting the text)	Shift+F3
Align text left	Ctrl+L
Align text centre	Ctrl+E
Align text right	Ctrl+R
Replace text	Ctrl+H
Find text	Ctrl+F
Print	Ctrl+P

Today I learned!

- Editing is the process of making changes to a document.
- Modifying the appearance of text is known as formatting.
- Formatting allows changes to be made to the font, size, type and style.
- The Thesaurus feature on MS Word allows us to use the synonyms for any word.
- Selecting the Line Alignment allows us to shift the text to the left, centre or right margin.
- Line spacing refers to space between lines.
- Paragraph spacing refers to space between paragraphs.
- MS Word has a Preview option that helps us see how the document would look before printing.
- Keyboard shortcuts help us save time while working on a document.

Revise and polish!

Learning Skills

1. Tick (✔) the correct answer.

a. Which of the following is used to move a copied text?

(i) Paste ☐ (ii) Stick ☐

(iii) Seal ☐ (iv) Move ☐

b. Which of the following options is used to increase the space between lines?

(i) Line Height ☐ (ii) Line Width ☐

(iii) Line Spacing ☐ (iv) Line Gap ☐

c. Which of the following options helps one find synonyms for words in MS Word?

(i) Dictionary ☐ (ii) Thesaurus ☐

(iii) Spell Check ☐ (iv) Find and Replace ☐

d. Which of the following is the keyboard shortcut to cut text?

(i) Ctrl+X ☐ (ii) Ctrl+C ☐

(iii) Ctrl+V ☐ (iv) Ctrl+M ☐

e. Which of the following features of MS Word points out the correct spelling of a misspelled word?

(i) Automatic spell checker ☐ (ii) Thesaurus ☐

(iii) Dictionary ☐ (iv) Spelling corrector ☐

2. Fill in the blanks using the given words.

editing synonyms Ctrl+F Ctrl+Z font

a. The process of making changes in a document is called ______________.

b. We can change the style of text by changing its ______________.

c. Thesaurus option can be used to find the ______________ for any word.

d. ______________ is the keyboard shortcut to undo an action.

e. ______________ is the keyboard shortcut to find text.

3. Match the following.

a.	Bold	(i)	A font type
b.	Italic	(ii)	CV Raman was a great scientist.
c.	Underline	(iii)	**The ice-cream is flavourful.**
d.	Times New Roman	(iv)	*The cool breeze is pleasant.*
e.	Highlighted text	(v)	The game was exciting!

4. Write down the keyboard shortcuts for the following actions.

a. Cut ___________ b. Copy ___________

c. Paste ___________ d. Undo ___________

e. Redo ___________ f. Bold ___________

g. Italic ___________ h. Underline ___________

5. Answer the following questions.

a. Explain editing with the help of an example.

b. Explain the importance of formatting.

c. What is meant by Thesaurus in MS Word?

d. How does spellcheck work in MS Word?

e. What are the steps to set the line spacing to 1 on MS Word?

Experiential Learning

Lab Activities

1. Create a document containing the names of five flowers you have seen in your neighbourhood, school or parks. Change the font colour of each flower name to the colour of the flower.
2. Create a document with the names of the Seven Wonders of the World. Highlight all the seven names with the seven colours of the rainbow.
3. Create a document with two paragraphs describing your favourite game. Highlight the parts you think are important.
4. Using the Thesaurus option in MS Word, find the synonyms of the following words:

   a. Splendid b. Joyous

   c. Moments d. Special

   e. Blessing

Chapter 4

The Internet—Web Browser

After reading this chapter, I will be able to:

- ✔ Label the parts of a browser window.
- ✔ Define the terminologies related to the internet network.
- ✔ Use appropriate keywords to collect information.
- ✔ Use the web responsibly while browsing.

Technology Literacy

Brainstorm and explore!

Fill in the blanks using the words given below.

website homepage keywords webpage

1. A ____________ contains text, images, videos and links to other webpages.
2. A ____________ is a collection of webpages on the internet that contains specific information.
3. The first page of a website is a ____________.
4. We can search for information using ____________ or images.

The internet connects millions of computers across the world. Computer users can exchange information with each other via the internet.

Computer Network

A network can be defined as an arrangement of interconnected people or things. Networks are very powerful because they enable communication, sharing of resources and allow an overall system to work smoothly.

A computer network is a set of computers that are connected to each other and share resources.

Brush up!

Consider communication between Rahul and Riddhi over a network. Rahul can send messages to Riddhi, to which she can reply using their respective computers. With two computers, they can send at least two messages. If their friend Kiran also joins the network, what would be the least number of messages?

____

Important Terms Related to the Internet

Let us look at some important terms related to the internet.

World Wide Web

The World Wide Web was invented by a British scientist named Tim Berners-Lee in 1989 (Fig. 4.1). It was originally created for enabling communication among scientists and was later made available to the public in 1991.

Fig. 4.1 | *Tim Berners-Lee*

Soak up!

The invention or the creation of the internet cannot be attributed to a single person. It is a series of multiple inventions by engineers, scientists and programmers that has led to the internet's widespread adoption and use.

The World Wide Web or www is a subset of the internet. Commonly called the web, it is a collection of web pages or websites, which is used by millions of people daily. These web pages are stored on **web servers** and connected to local computers through the internet via **web browsers**.

www is a collection of web pages over the internet.

The World Wide Web consortium, or W3C, is an international organization or community that develops and maintains the WWW standards. Its objective is to make sure the World Wide Web works at its best by developing and ensuring guidelines and protocols for the users and companies to follow.

Web Servers

We have a cupboard to store all our clothes. Similarly, web servers are computers that store web pages. These web servers are owned by a web host that allocates space to every website (Fig. 4.2).

Small websites either store all their web pages on a single server or part of a server. Big websites or organizations store their web pages on different servers (often) in different countries.

Fig. 4.2 | *Web server*

Soak up!

Servers are huge in size. They are capable of storing large amounts of data and performing complex calculations. This is why, servers generate a lot of heat. Companies spend a lot of money to ensure that the server rooms do not get overheated. Overheating can damage the servers, causing physical damage and loss of data.

Internet Service Provider

Devices, such as personal computers, laptops and smartphones connect to the internet with the help of Wi-Fi technology. A router or set of routers is installed in homes, schools, offices, etc., which give the Wi-Fi signals. An internet service provider (ISP) provides services, such as installing broadband cables and routers in a particular area (Fig. 4.3).

Fig. 4.3 | *Different users connected to a Wi-Fi network*

A router helps us connect multiple devices to each other and to the internet.

URL

We now know that a web page is stored on a web server. A web server can contain multiple websites or web pages. How can we locate these web pages? We use the address of a person to locate the person in a city. Similarly, websites also have an address that is used to locate them on the World Wide Web.

In simpler terms, uniform resource locator (URL) is the online address assigned to a web page.

The address assigned to a web page/web document is called the uniform resource locator (URL) or the website address.

A URL comprises three major parts: protocol, domain name and path. For example,

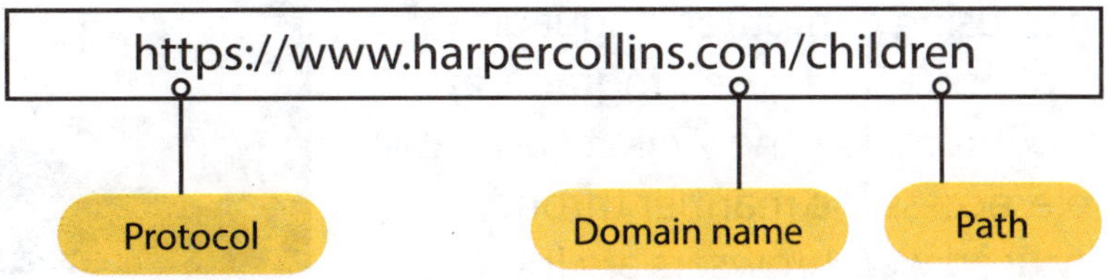

Let us see the function of each part:

1. The **protocol** is a set of rules that tell a web browser how to communicate with the web server when accessing a website or sending any information. The most common protocol used today is the **https** (hypertext transfer protocol secure). The https protocol ensures that all the information exchanged is encrypted by the web browser.

2. The **domain name** is what a user types on the web browser address bar to access the website. Any person, business or organization requires a unique domain name before creating their website.

   In the above example, *.com* is the name of the domain.

3. We know that we need to define the path in a computer to locate a specific file or folder. Similarly, on the internet, the domain **path** name is used to locate a web directory or file on a web server. In the example, *harpercollins* is the name of the folder and *children* is the name of the file to be retrieved.

Some popular domain names and their uses are given in Table 4.1.

Table 4.1 | *Popular domain names and their uses*

Domain name	Use
.com	Used for commercial websites, for example, www.amazon.com
.org	Used to represent organizations (mostly non-profit), for example, www.cry.org
.gov	Used to represent government institutions, for example, www.mhrd.gov.in is the official website of India's Ministry of Human Resource Development
.edu	Used by educational companies, for example, www.isb.edu is one of India's famous management institutes
.net	Intended for network organizations, such as internet service providers
.mil	Used to represent military websites
.in	Used to represent websites of Indian companies, for example, www.collins.in is one of the companies based in India

Web Browser

A web browser, or simply 'browser', is a software application used to access websites (Fig. 4.4). Websites or web pages are written using computer languages, such as HTML, JavaScript and CSS. These programs are translated by a browser. This makes the website available to the user in a readable, accessible manner through its window. Commonly used web browsers are Internet Explorer, Google Chrome, Safari and Mozilla Firefox.

Fig. 4.4 | *Web browser*

Soak up!

The first web browser was named WorldWideWeb, which was later changed to Nexus to avoid confusion. It was also created by Tim Berners-Lee in 1990.

Crank up! Technology Literacy

A lot of websites may not appear the same way in every browser due to the differences between browsers.

Parts of a Browser Window

A browser is one of the most frequently used applications on a computer. Therefore, it is intuitive and simple to use. Figure 4.5 shows the main parts of the Microsoft Edge web browser window.

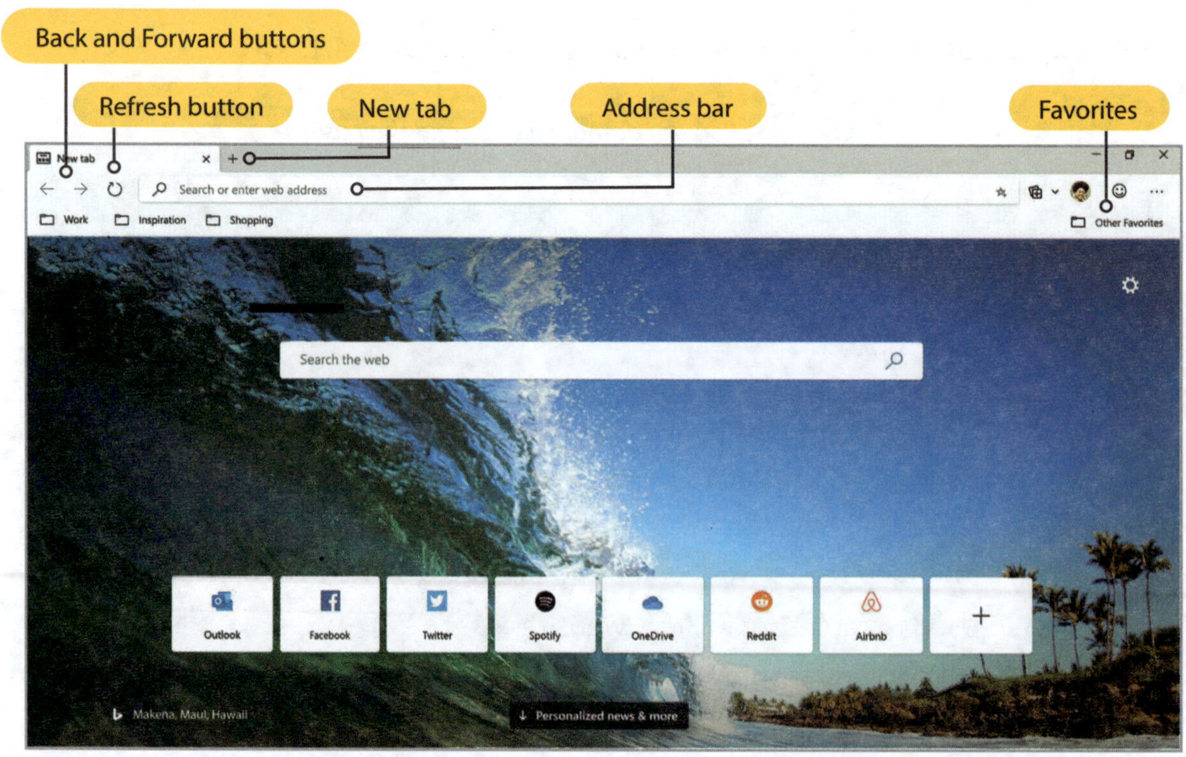

Fig. 4.5 | *Parts of a browser window*

These are the parts of a browser window:

- **Address Bar**: This part of the browser allows users to enter the URL of a website. The **Address bar** displays a website URL the user is currently on.
- **Refresh Button**: This button reloads the contents of the current website with the latest data.
- **Favorites**: The user can save their favourite websites or the ones they need to refer back to using the **Favorites** option. To save a page as favourite, simply click on the **Add this page to favorites** button next to the address bar.
- **Back and Forward Buttons**: The **Back button** takes the user to the previous webpage of the current website the user has visited. The **Forward button** reverses the action of the back button and takes the user to the next page visited.
- **New Tab**: A tab is a feature of the web browser that allows the user to open and browse a webpage. The **New tab** option allows the user to open a new tab. Multiple tabs can be opened at once.

Link up!

Browser extensions are applications that can be installed on a browser to enhance or modify its functionality.

Search Engines

Leena is creating a project for the semester exams. Help her find the following information.

- Which is the biggest flower in the world?
- What is the total number of galaxies discovered so far?
- Give the history of the Olympic games.
- Name the tributaries of the Ganges river.

In all of the above instances, Leena will use the internet to search for the information.

Whenever we search for a term over the internet, we get relevant information about it within a fraction of a second. The application or software that helps us search the information over the internet is called **search engine**. The most popular search engines are Google, Microsoft Bing and Yahoo.

A search engine is a software that searches the World Wide Web for information and returns the results to the users.

Searching for a term over the internet is a three-step process, as discussed below:

Step 1: The user enters the search term.

Step 2: The search engine scans its list of indexed website for the searched word.

Step 3: The search engine displays the result in the order of relevance.

With the help of a search engine, users can learn almost everything at the click of a button.

Access to information was not always this fast. Before the tool to search information on the internet was created, humans had to access this knowledge through books and by visiting libraries.

Link up!

The process of adjusting the content, structure, etc., of a website so that it is displayed prominently by a search engine is known as the search engine optimization (SEO). SEO makes a website more visible to user and thus results in increased traffic to it.

Brush up!

List names of search engines apart from the ones mentioned in the chapter.

____

____

Keywords

Let us help Leena search the required information on the internet.

- Which is the biggest flower in the world?
- What is the total number of galaxies discovered so far?
- Give the history of the Olympic games.
- Name the tributaries of the Ganges river.

In the context of computers, the words or terms used in order to search for information on the internet are known as keywords.

The underlined words represent the **keywords** Leena has used to search for information on the internet.

Website designers try to determine the terms that users would use to search for information on their website and include those terms in a strategic manner on their website. This is known as **search engine optimization**.

The steps to search for information (in a strategic manner) on the internet are as follows:

Step 1: Ensure the systems/device is connected to the internet.

Step 2: Open the search engine of your choice.

Step 3: Enter the keyword(s).

Step 4: Click on the **Search** button or press the **Enter** key on the keyboard.

Technology Literacy

Crank up!

Here are some tricks we can use to make our search more effective:

1. **Double quotes (" ")**: Use the exact phrase that you are looking for. Insert quotes " " before and after the phrase. For example, if you are looking for *search engines*, type "*search engines*" in the search bar.
2. **Minus (–) sign**: To exclude a keyword, use the minus (–) sign before the keyword. For example, if you are looking for a list of search engines that shows all the search engines other than *Google*, type "*search engines-google*" in the search bar.
3. **Asterisk (*) sign**: This sign does two things:
   (i) If used between a phrase, * helps the search engine find the missing word. For example, if you type *the most * search engines*, you will see the alternatives to the * as *used*, *popular*, *famous*, etc.
   (ii) If used after a phrase, * helps the search engine complete a phrase. For example, if you type *search engines**, you can see the alternatives to the * as *available today*, *and their advantages*, *are used for*, etc.

Fun with AI

Search engines use algorithms powered by Artificial Intelligence to make searches faster and more relevant. They also use AI to autocomplete and autocorrect the keywords.

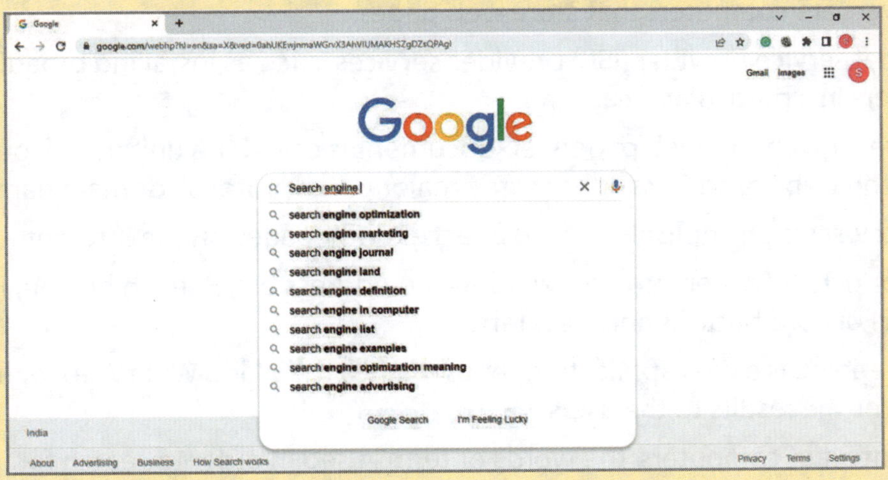

Safe Browsing

The internet is a very vast repository of information. As it grows, there is a higher chance of it being misused. Web browsers use encryption to ensure the safety of users. With access to information on our fingertips, we also need to judiciously use the internet. Following are some of the steps one can take to remain safe online:

> Net surfing or web surfing or browsing means looking through different web pages on the internet.

1. Do not set an easy password. Try to use different passwords for different websites.
2. Do not share your password with anyone.
3. Shop only from secure sites. Check that the URL has the *https* protocol (instead of *http*).
4. Do not click on pop-ups.
5. Be careful while using public Wi-Fi.

encryption: system for security and fraud prevention, which automatically breaks up and reorders information before it is sent via telephone lines or the internet

6. Do not click on random links sent by strangers via emails or online gaming sites.

Today I learned!

- A network can be defined as an arrangement of interconnected people or things.
- A computer network is a set of computers that are connected to each other and share resources.
- WWW stands for World Wide Web and is a collection of webpages over the internet.
- Web servers are computers that store web pages.
- An internet service provider (ISP) provides services, such as installing broadband cables and routers in a particular area.
- The address given to a web page/web document is called the uniform resource locator (URL) or the website address. It has three major parts: protocol, domain name and path.
- A web browser is an application used to access web pages on the internet.
- The major parts of a web browser window are Address bar, Refresh button, Favorites, Back and Forward buttons and New tab.
- A search engine is a web application that searches the World Wide Web for information and returns the results to the users.
- In the context of computers, the words or terms used in order to search for information on the internet are known as keywords.
- Web browsers use encryption to ensure safety of users.
- It is important to practice responsible behaviour while using the internet.

Revise and polish!

Learning Skills

1. Tick (✔) the correct answer.

a. Which of the following contains the address of a website?

(i) Uniform redirect locator ☐ (ii) Uniform resource location ☐

(iii) Unified resource location ☐ (iv) Uniform resource locator ☐

b. Which of the following displays the website URL the user is currently on?

(i) Favorites ☐ (ii) Forward button ☐

(iii) Refresh button ☐ (iv) Address bar ☐

c. Google and Microsoft Bing are examples of:

(i) Browsers ☐ (ii) Search engines ☐

(iii) Websites ☐ (iv) Web pages ☐

d. Google Chrome, Microsoft Edge and Mozilla Firefox are examples of:

(i) Browsers ☐ (ii) Search engines ☐

(iii) Websites ☐ (iv) Web pages ☐

e. Which of the following is a part of the URL?

(i) Protocol ☐ (ii) Domain name ☐

(iii) Path ☐ (iv) All of the above ☐

2. Fill in the blanks using the given words.

password Keywords network World Wide Web internet

a. A computer user can exchange any information with another computer user via the _______________.

b. WWW stands for _______________.

c. A _______________ is a set of connected computers that share resources.

d. _______________ are terms or words used to look for information on a search engine.

e. The _______________ for an email or social media account should be difficult to crack and should not be shared with anyone.

3. Match the following.

a.	ISP	(i)	Keywords
b.	www	(ii)	Uniform resource locator
c.	URL	(iii)	World Wide Web
d.	Browser	(iv)	Internet service provider
e.	Search engine	(v)	Microsoft Bing

4. Answer the following questions.

a. Write a short note on computer networks.

b. Write a short note on URLs.

c. What are search engines and how do they work?

d. What are keywords?

e. What is encryption and where is it used?

5. Categorize the following into safe and unsafe practices while using the internet:

a. Setting the password of your email account as *abcde*

b. Avoiding clicking an unknown link on the internet

c. Clicking on pop-ups

d. Browsing a website with the URL http://www.xyz.com

e. Opening links from trustworthy sources

Safe	Unsafe

Lab Activity

Experiential Learning

We have learned about the Microsoft Edge web browser. Other browsers, such as Google Chrome, Mozilla Firefox and Safari are also widely used. In addition to technical differences, they are different in their look and feel. Download the Chrome browser on your computer. Find and label the following parts:

- Address bar
- Refresh button
- Back and Forward buttons
- New tab

Chapter

5

Presentation Software— An Introduction

After reading this chapter, I will be able to:

- ✔ Explain the purpose of presentation software.
- ✔ Choose appropriate layouts according to the requirement.
- ✔ Describe the components of a presentation software window.
- ✔ Create and add text and images to a slide.
- ✔ Navigate between slides.
- ✔ Present a slide show.

Brainstorm and explore!

Cross Curricular

Krish has to explain the addition of numbers to his friend with an example. Which of the following ways should he use to make it interesting?

The process of adding two numbers is known as addition. If I have 1 apple and you have 2 apples, then the total number of apples is 1 + 2 = 3.

MS Word allows users to insert both pictures and text in a document. However, there are times when we want to present information in a simpler and more effective way, such as presenting a project or teaching a classroom in a fun and interesting way.

MS PowerPoint

MS PowerPoint is a software application used to make presentations. PowerPoint was first released in the year 1987. There have been many versions of PowerPoint since then. In this chapter, we will learn about MS PowerPoint 2016.

Microsoft PowerPoint is a computer application from the Microsoft Office suite used to design presentations.

presentation: a collection of slides arranged in a systematic order to display the information along with graphics, sound and animation. A slide is like a page in a PowerPoint presentation that displays some information about a topic

Soak up!

PowerPoint was originally invented by Robert Gaskins and was later bought by Microsoft.

Uses of Presentation Software

Presentation software is useful in many ways. Some of these are discussed here:

1. Business people make presentations to display their products or services to customers, clients and/or managers.
2. Teachers use presentations for effective teaching in the classroom.
3. Presentations are normally used to attract large audience in a meeting or a conference.
4. Presentations can also be used to inform or educate a large gathering.

Starting MS PowerPoint 2016

There are two ways to start the MS PowerPoint application on our computer.

Click the **Start** button and then select **PowerPoint** (Fig. 5.1).

OR

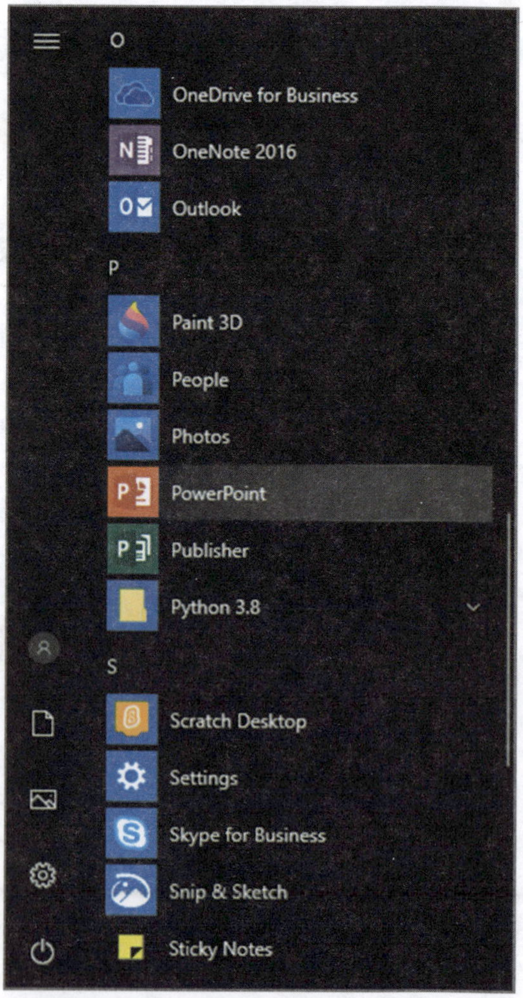

Fig. 5.1 | *Opening MS PowerPoint using the Start button*

Click the **Search bar** on the bottom-left of the screen and type **PowerPoint** in the search bar the press the **Enter** key on the keyboard (Fig. 5.2).

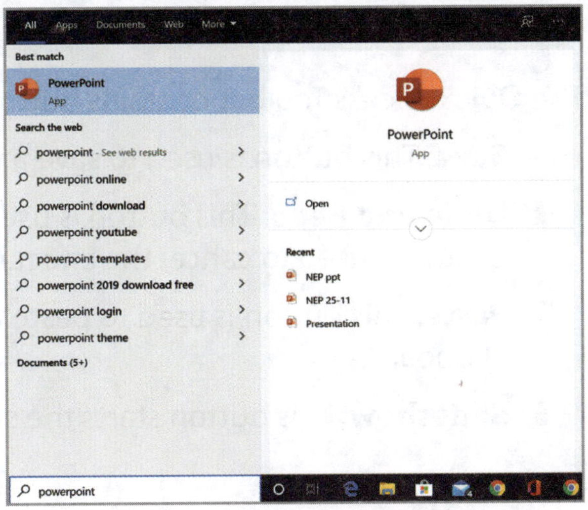

Fig. 5.2 | *Opening PowerPoint*

Parts of the MS PowerPoint Window

After starting MS PowerPoint, select the **Blank Presentation** option. It will display a window, as shown in Fig. 5.3.

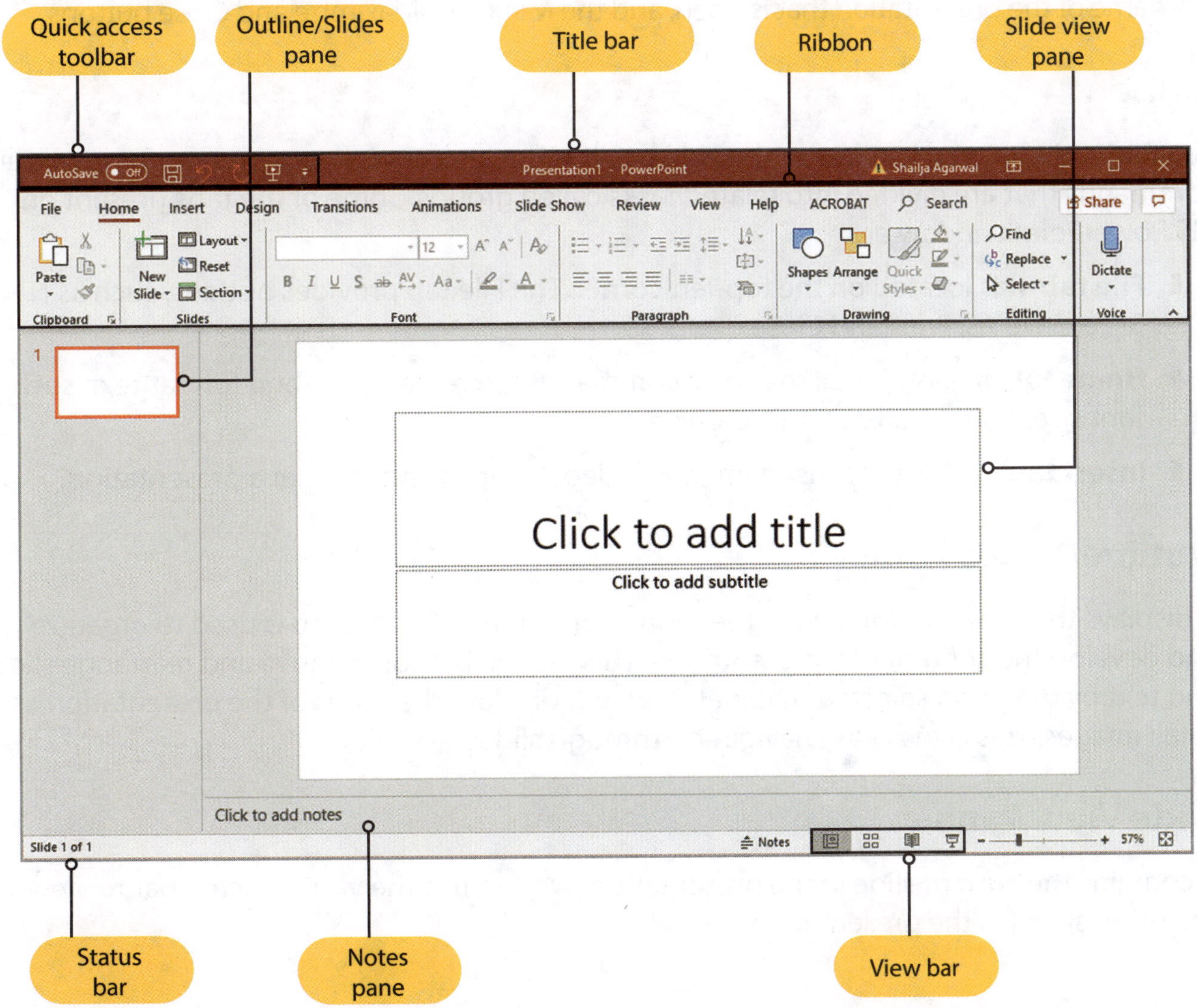

Fig. 5.3 | *Parts of the MS PowerPoint window*

Let us discuss these parts in detail.

Quick Access Toolbar

The Quick Access Toolbar contains buttons for commonly used commands.

- **Save**: This button is used to save a file.
- **Undo and Redo**: This button is used to undo the last change that was made. The Redo button is used to cancel the effect of the Undo button.
- **Paste**: This button is used to paste anything that have been copied or cut onto the clipboard.
- **Slideshow**: This button starts the slide-by-slide presentation of the project.

Title Bar

The Title bar is present at the top of the window. It indicates the name of the software program, the name of the presentation that is open, and the Minimize, Maximize and Close buttons.

Ribbon

The Ribbon is located just below the Title bar. It is the area containing the tabs. Tabs contain commands that are divided into related tasks called groups. Some of the tabs present on MS PowerPoint window are:

- **File tab**: It is located on the top-left corner. The File tab provides options, such as New, Save, Save As, Print and Close.
- **Home tab**: It contains all the basic commands to create a slide and format text, such as font size, styles, bullets, font colour, etc.
- **Insert tab**: It is used to insert images, videos, shapes and icons in a presentation.

Outline/Slides Pane

It displays the presentation text in the form of an outline. Outline tab is used to organize and develop the content of a presentation. This tab enables us to move and rearrange slides and text by dragging selected material. Slide tab displays the slides of the presentation as small images. This allows easy navigation through slides.

Slide View Pane

It contains the current slide in the presentation. We can use the vertical scroll bar to view the other slides in the presentation.

Status Bar

Located at the bottom-left corner of the window, it displays the number of slides and the current slide number.

Notes Pane

It is located below the Slide pane. It is used to type reference notes for the speaker. The notes can be printed and referred to during the presentation.

View Bar

It is located at the bottom right-hand side of the screen. It contains buttons that allow the users to switch between PowerPoint views. The first view is called the **Normal** view, and it is the default view of MS PowerPoint. The second view is called **Slide Sorter** view. It shows all the slides in sequence for us to see. The third view is called the **Reader View**, and it shows the presentation one slide at a time. The fourth view is called the **Slide Show** view. It shows how each slide would look during a presentation.

Working with Presentations

Let us learn how to work with presentations in MS PowerPoint 2016.

Creating a New Presentation

Just like we use MS Word to create documents, MS PowerPoint is used to create presentations (Fig. 5.4). To create a new presentation, follow the steps given below:

1. Select the **File** tab on the top-left corner.
2. Click the **New** option.
3. Click on the **Blank Presentation** option.

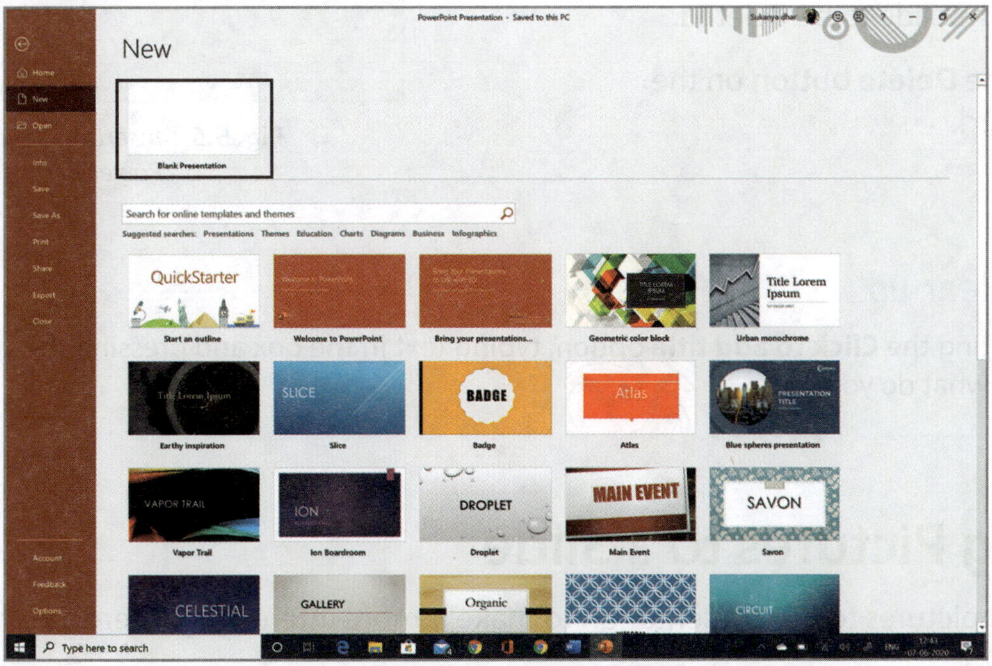

Fig. 5.4 | *New presentation in MS PowerPoint*

Inserting and Deleting a Slide

In a presentation, we will have to insert multiple slides to make it more interesting and detailed (Fig. 5.5). To insert a new slide, follow the steps given below:

1. Under the **Insert** tab, select the arrow below **New** slide.
2. Select a layout from the options and create a **New Slide**.

A layout in presentation is the structure or format of each slide in the deck.

Technology Literacy

Crank up!

To create a new presentation, the keyboard shortcut is Ctrl+N.

To delete a slide, follow the steps given below:

1. Select the slide to be deleted.
2. Press the **Delete** button on the keyboard.

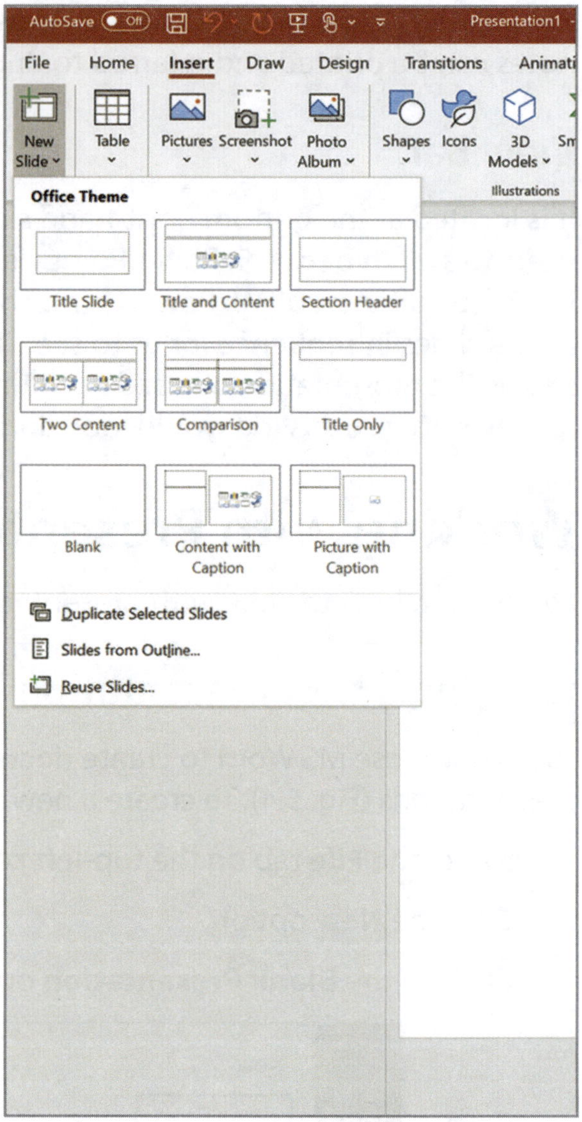

Fig. 5.5 | *Inserting a slide in MS PowerPoint*

Clear up!

After selecting the **Click to add title** option, typing text in the box and pressing the **Enter** key, what do you see?

Adding Pictures to a Slide

We can add pictures to our presentation to make it more interesting. There are many ways to do this.

Inserting Pictures from a File

The steps for inserting pictures from file are given below:

1. Select the slide in which the image needs to be added.
2. Select **Insert** → **Picture** → **This Device**... option, as shown in Fig. 5.6.
3. Choose the picture and click **Insert**.

The picture will appear in the selected slide.

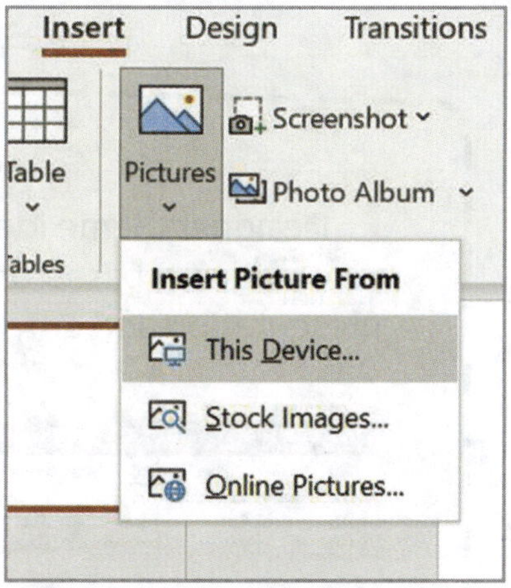

Fig. 5.6 | *Inserting pictures using This Device option*

Inserting Online Pictures

The steps for inserting pictures online are given below:

1. Select the slide in which the image is to be added.
2. Select **Insert** → **Picture** → **Online Pictures**... option (Fig. 5.7).

Fig. 5.7 | *Online Pictures option under the Pictures option*

3. The **Online Pictures** dialog box appears (Fig. 5.8). Search for the image by giving the exact keyword in the search box and press the **Enter** key.

Fig. 5.8 | *Inserting online pictures into PowerPoint presentations*

4. Select a picture from the search results and click **Insert**.

The picture will appear in the selected slide.

Fun with AI

Designer theme ideas is a way PowerPoint is helping the users choose a layout automatically based on the theme of the user's presentation. When you open a blank presentation and enter words onto the slide, Designer's AI chooses the most suitable layouts automatically for the content.

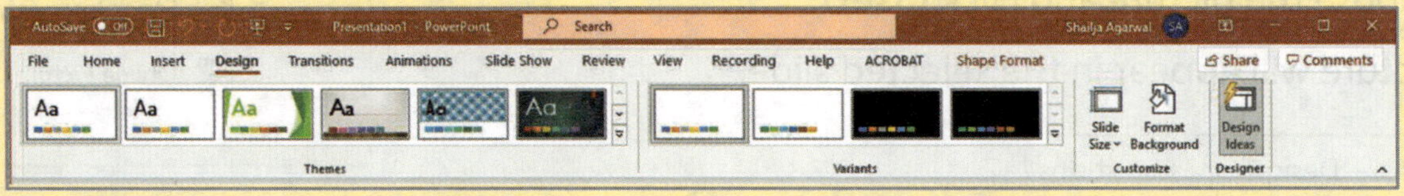

PowerPoint has added live captioning and multilingual subtitle features using AI, which make it easy for audiences to understand the presentation. This is extremely useful when the audience is unable to understand the language being used by the presenter.

Link up!

Before the introduction to PowerPoint and modern projectors, an overhead projector was used to make presentations. An overhead projector is a machine that has light inside it and can be used to make the writing or pictures on a thin sheet of plastic appear on a screen or a wall. The sheets were called acetate sheets or transparencies. These sheets were made up of a transparent, flexible material.

Slide Layouts

MS PowerPoint allows us to select a layout from multiple layout templates available (Fig. 5.9).

1. The **Title Slide** layout is the default layout of a blank presentation in PowerPoint. It comprises two text placeholders: the first for the presentation title and the second for a subtitle.

placeholder: a box that holds text and graphics, such as pictures, ClipArt, tables, charts, etc.

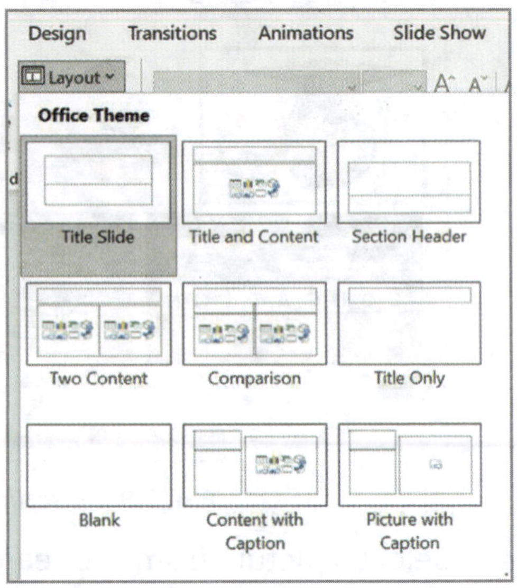

Fig. 5.9 | *Slide Layout drop down menu*

2. The **Title and Content** layout is the most commonly-used layout. It comprises a title placeholder and a content placeholder.
3. The **Section Header** layout is ideal for slides that introduce new sections within the presentation. It includes two placeholders: a title placeholder and a text placeholder.
4. The **Two Content** layout has a title placeholder and two content placeholders that appear side-by-side.
5. The **Comparison** layout has a title placeholder, two text placeholders and two content placeholders.
6. The **Title Only** layout is the same as a Title Slide except that it does not have a subtitle placeholder.
7. The **Blank** has nothing written on it. It is completely blank.
8. The **Content with Caption** layout has a title and caption placeholder on the left and a content placeholder on the right.
9. The **Picture with Caption** layout has a title placeholder, a caption placeholder and a placeholder for images.

Running a Slide Show

Once the presentation is prepared, it is time to run it. To run a slide show, select the **Slide Show** tab on the Ribbon (Fig. 5.10).

Fig. 5.10 | *Slide Show tab*

The **Slide Show** tab comprises the **Start Slide Show** group with four options as follows:

- 

: This option starts the slide show from the beginning.
- 

: This option starts the slide show from the current slide that is selected on the presentation.
- 

: This option allows us to select a service to present the slide show online.

- 

: This option allows us to select the slides that need to be shown in the presentation. The slides can be selected based on the audience as what we want them to see. We can hide slides from the slides by selecting the **Slide Hide** option from **Set Up** group under the **Slide Show** tab.

Clear up!

Explore what the other options in the **Set Up** group under the **Slide Show** tab does.

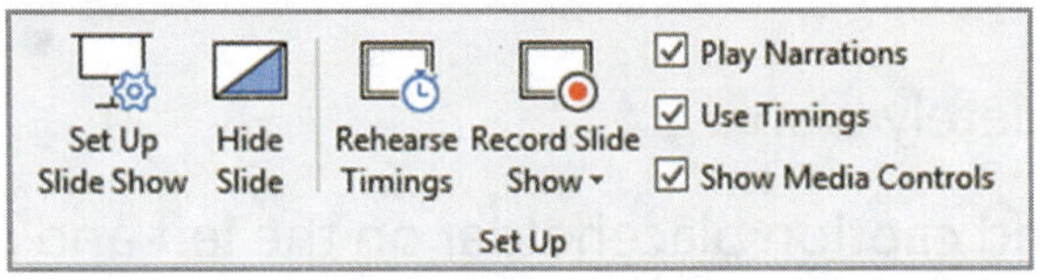

Soak up!

A presenter reading from PowerPoint slides is the most annoying thing rated by the audience. In order to gain the audience's attention, add pointers to the presentation and never try to read out what is already written in the presentation.

Saving a Presentation

Now that a new presentation has been created, it is time to save it. To save a presentation, follow the steps given below:

1. Select the **File** tab and click the **Save As** option.
2. Select the location to save the file.
3. Type the file name in the field **Enter file name here** and click on **Save**. The file is saved with a **.pptx** extension (Fig. 5.11).

Soak up!

Every second, more than 350 PowerPoint presentations are begun around the world. This makes about 30,000,000 presentations in total per day.

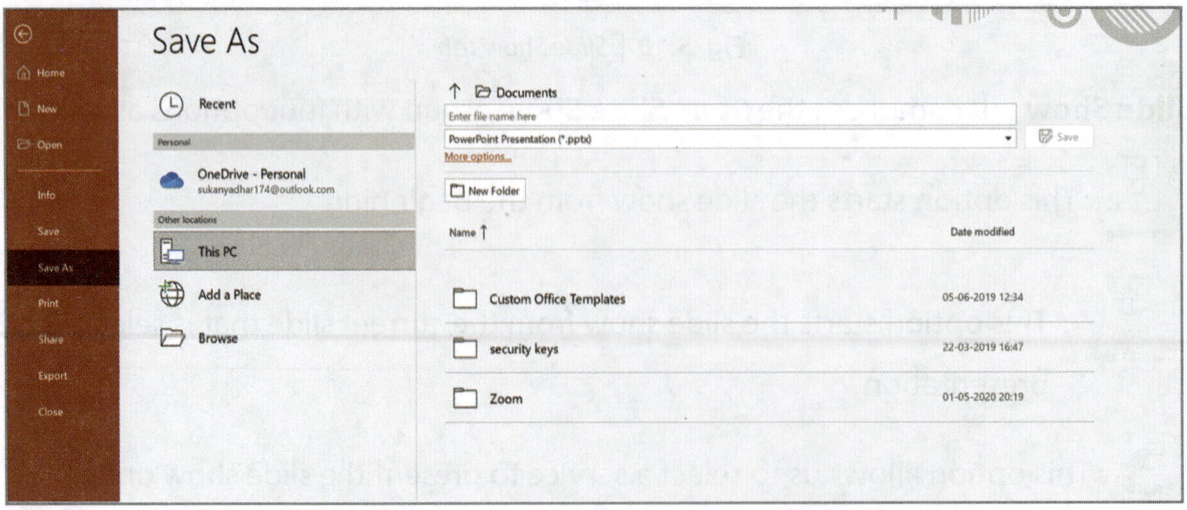

Fig. 5.11 | *Saving a presentation in MS PowerPoint*

Opening an Existing Presentation

The easiest way to open an existing presentation is by double-clicking the file where it is saved. The steps to open it from the MS PowerPoint application window are given below:

1. Click on the **File** tab and then select **Open** option.
2. Search the folder location and select the file to be opened.
3. Click on the **Open** button. The presentation will open (Fig. 5.12).

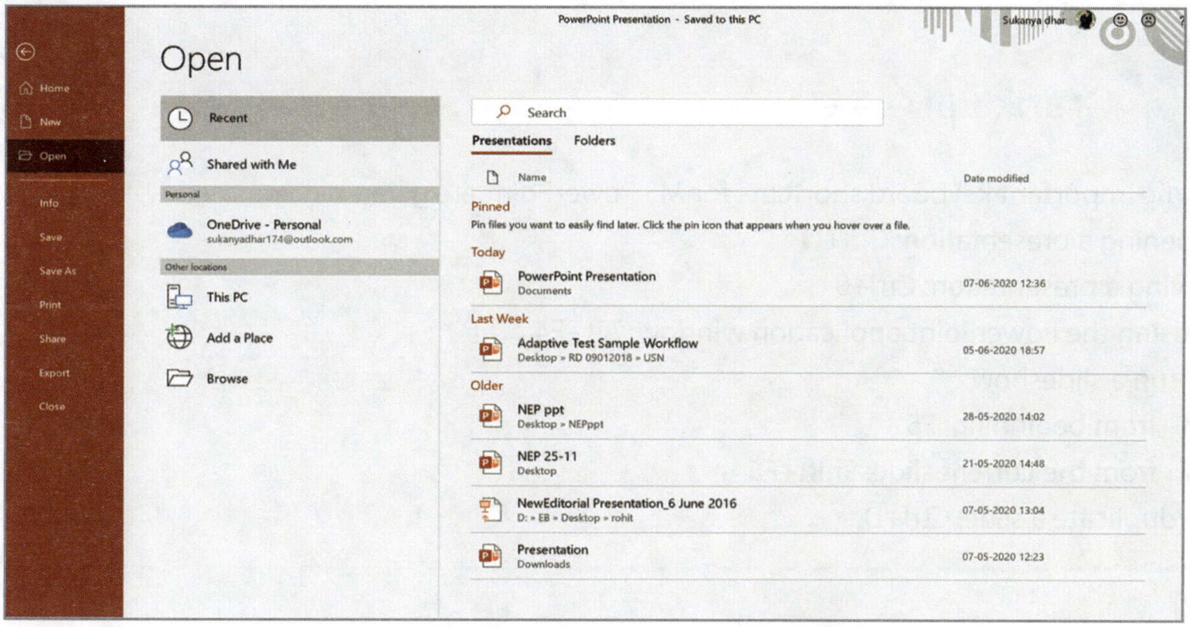

Fig. 5.12 | *Opening a presentation in MS PowerPoint*

Closing a Presentation

To close a presentation, follow the steps given below:

1. Select the **File** Tab on the top-left corner.
2. Click on the **Close** option.

Exiting MS PowerPoint

To Exit MS PowerPoint, click on the **Close** (X) button on the top-right corner of the screen (Fig. 5.13).

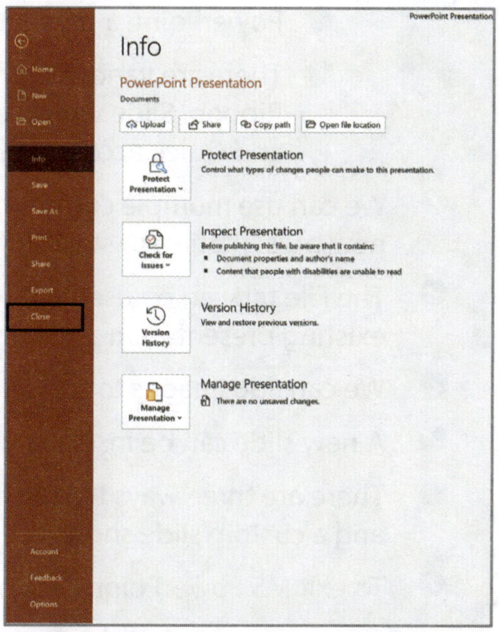

Fig. 5.13 | *Closing a presentation*

Brush up!

Guess who am I?

1. I display the name of the software application and file currently in use. ______________
2. I play your slides as an actual presentation. ______________
3. I display the notes created by the speaker for the content in the slide pane. ______________

Crank up!

Technology Literacy

Some important keyboard shortcuts for MS PowerPoint are given below:

Opening a presentation: Ctrl+O

Saving a presentation: Ctrl+S

Closing the PowerPoint application window: Alt+F4

To run a slideshow

- from beginning: F5
- from the current slide: Shift+F5

To duplicate a slide: Ctrl+D

Today I learned!

- PowerPoint, a presentation program, is part of Microsoft Office suite.
- There are various components in PowerPoint window. Some of these are Title bar, Ribbon, Slide view pane, Notes pane, Outline/Slides pane, Status bar, View bar and Quick access toolbar.
- We can use multiple commands from the Quick access toolbar to open, save and create a new presentation or start slideshow.
- The File tab can be used to create a new presentation, save a presentation, open an existing presentation and close the presentation.
- We can add images to the slides from saved pictures or search for them on the internet.
- A new slide can be inserted using the Insert tab.
- There are three ways to start a slide show—from the beginning, from the current slide and a custom slide show.
- To exit MS PowerPoint, click on the Close (X) button on the top-right corner of the screen.

Revise and polish!

Learning Skills

1. Tick (✓) the correct answer.

a. Which button is used to cancel the effect of the Undo button?

(i) Copy ☐ (ii) Paste ☐ (iii) Cut ☐ (iv) Redo ☐

b. A new slide can be inserted using the ____________ tab.

(i) File ☐ (ii) Insert ☐ (iii) View ☐ (iv) Review ☐

c. Which toolbar comprises Save, Undo and Paste options?

(i) Quick Access ☐ (ii) Backstage ☐

(iii) Insert ☐ (iv) Title bar ☐

d. ____________ is used to create presentations.

(i) MS Excel ☐ (ii) MS PowerPoint ☐

(iii) MS Access ☐ (iv) All of these ☐

e. Which of these options is used to run a slide show?

(i) Slide Play ☐ (ii) Slide View ☐

(iii) Slide Show ☐ (iv) Title Slide ☐

f. The Save As option is present in the ____________ tab.

(i) Insert ☐ (ii) Review ☐

(iii) File ☐ (iv) View ☐

g. Which of these is the easiest way to open an existing presentation?

(i) Double-clicking the file ☐ (ii) Copying the file ☐

(iii) Printing the file ☐ (iv) All of these ☐

h. Which of the following is used to see all the slides at once?

(i) Slide Sorter view ☐ (ii) Slide view ☐

(iii) Normal view ☐ (iv) All of the above ☐

i. To hide a slide, this option is used:

(i) Slide Hide ☐ (ii) Slide delete ☐

(iii) Slide Show ☐ (iv) All of the above ☐

j. To close a presentation, select the ____________ option under the File tab.

(i) Close ☐ (ii) Print ☐

(iii) Play ☐ (iv) Stop ☐

2. Fill in the blanks using the given words.

Home .pptx placeholders Ctrl+O Ctrl+N

a. ______________ is the keyboard shortcut to open a new presentation in MS PowerPoint.

b. A new slide can be inserted using the ______________ tab.

c. A presentation is saved with ______________ extension.

d. In PowerPoint, the objects on the slide used to hold the text are called ______________.

e. The shortcut key to open an existing presentation is ______________.

3. Match the following.

a.	Saving a presentation	(i)	Alt+F4
b.	Closing a presentation	(ii)	F5
c.	Opening a new slide	(iii)	Ctrl+S
d.	To run a slideshow from beginning	(iv)	Ctrl+M

4. State whether the following statements are true (T) or false (F).

a. Notes pane helps to add notes to each slide separately. ☐

b. To insert a new slide in a presentation, we first click the Insert tab. ☐

c. You click inside the placeholder to type in it. ☐

d. The Pictures option is available in the Design tab. ☐

e. On clicking the File tab, a full screen File menu appears. It is also known as Quick access toolbar. ☐

5. Answer the following questions.

a. What is Microsoft PowerPoint?

b. What are the different parts of the MS PowerPoint window?

c. How to create a new presentation in MS PowerPoint?

d. How to save a presentation in MS PowerPoint?

e. What are the two ways to close a presentation in MS PowerPoint?

Lab Activities

Experiential Learning

1. Create a presentation that consists of two slides.

   Slide 1: use title layout,

   Title: "My Hobbies", Subtitle: "Your name".

   Slide 2: use title and content layout.

   Mention all your hobbies with the help of some pictures.

2. Design a presentation on your favourite destination. Ensure that you include some of the famous places to visit and recommended food of your destination in your presentation. Present it using slide show in front of the class.

3. Create a friends magazine containing descriptions of all your friends, their role in your life and their photographs.

Chapter 6

Step-wise Thinking

After reading this chapter, I will be able to:

- ✔ Describe step-by-step thinking.
- ✔ Analyse a task and break it up into parts.
- ✔ Predict the possible solutions.

Brainstorm and explore!

Miss Ratna is the class teacher for Class 4, section A. It is the time of the year when she plans for the annual trip to the amusement park for the class. In her school, only one section can go on a picnic on a given day. Planning a picnic for 40 students is a difficult task but Miss Ratna has a very simple method to ensure it is carried out smoothly. Can you guess what the method is?

First, Miss Ratna breaks down the task of planning a picnic into very simple steps. These steps are: setting the date for the picnic, booking tickets for the amusement park and communicating the dates and venue to the parents.

Then, Miss Ratna further simplifies the task at hand by breaking down each step into sub-steps. She meticulously goes over each of them till all her planning is done! The approach used by Miss Ratna is known as **step-wise thinking**. This is shown in Table 6.1.

meticulous: very carefully and with great attention to detail

Table 6.1 | *Planning a school trip*

Step 1: Setting the date for the picnic. **Step 1.1**: Check the school calendar and exclude exam days and public holidays. **Step 1.2**: Check with other class teachers for any clashes. **Step 1.3**: Seek permission from the school.	**Step 2**: Booking tickets for the amusement park. **Step 2.1**: Look for the contact details of the amusement park from the internet or the school. **Step 2.2**: Call the amusement park officials and check for the date. **Step 2.3**: Confirm the booking.	**Step 3**: Communicating the dates and venue to the parents. **Step 3.1**: Prepare a message with date, time, venue and registration details. **Step 3.2**: Email the parents. **Step 3.3**: Resolving their queries.

What do you think will happen if Miss Ratna does not get tickets for the desired date (at step 2.2)?

Breaking down a task into smaller steps and arriving at possible solutions to achieve the desired goal is known as step-wise thinking.

Task/Problem → Break into smaller sub-problems → Find a solution

Clear up!

Miss Ratna has shared a roll number-wise list of students going for the picnic with Vishal. She has asked him to tick names of students going for the picnic. He also needs to make sure the students board the bus in a queue. Help Vishal break down this task into smaller steps.

____

____

____

____

Sequential Thinking

After dividing a task into simple steps, it is important to follow the steps in an orderly manner. This is called sequential thinking. For example, Miss Ratna cannot send a notice to the parents without setting the date.

We use sequential thinking in everyday life also. Let us discuss some real-life examples of sequential thinking.

1. **Counting numbers**: Numbers always follow a sequence. Suppose, we go to a shop to buy mangoes. By mistake, we count **four** instead of **three** and pay the price of **four** mangoes! We would be at a loss.

✔ 1	✔ 2	✔ 3	✔ 4
✔ 1	✔ 2	✘ 4	✘ 3
1	2	4	3

2. **Writing sentences**: Every sentence is made up of words in a particular order that makes sense. Read the sentences given below:

✔ The <u>cat</u> drinks the <u>milk</u>.	✘ The <u>milk</u> drinks the <u>cat</u>.

The sentence becomes incorrect if we change the positions of milk and cat. Thus, it is important to use words in the correct order for the sentence to have proper meaning.

3. **Doing everyday activities**: We do everyday activities in a sequential manner. If we miss any step, the task would not be completed.

Read the following steps Neeraj follows daily for getting ready for school. If he does not follow these in correct order, he will not be able to reach school on time.

✘	✔
1. Wake up 2. Rinse my mouth 3. Brush my teeth 4. Have breakfast 5. Wear school uniform 6. Take bath 7. Go to school?!	1. Wake up 2. Brush my teeth 3. Rinse my mouth 4. Take bath 5. Wear school uniform 6. Have breakfast 8. Go to school! 
I ate breakfast without rinsing my mouth and have a wet school uniform. I will not be allowed to enter the school!	I followed all the steps sequentially. I will reach school clean and well fed!

Brush up!

Correct the order of the following sequences. One has been done for you.

1. A B D C	A B C D
2. 5 4 2 3 1	
3. Morning Evening Afternoon Night	
4. I am a child good.	

Problem-solving and Reasoning

Read the following passage carefully. Spot and underline the errors.

Anand went to a supermarket and bought 2 oranges. On his way back, he spotted another fruit shop and bought 3 mangoes. He came home with 6 fruits in his hand. After eating 2 oranges and 1 mango, he is left with just 1 fruit.

Can you find some mistakes in the passage? Underline the errors.

While solving the example, we process the given information in our brain. We do logical calculations, such as:

- 2 apples + 3 mangoes = 5 fruits and find that the passage incorrectly mentions 6 fruits.
- After eating 2 oranges and 1 mango out of 5 fruits, Anand is left with 5 – (2 + 1) = 2 fruits.

We use reasoning skill to identify the problem at hand.

The action of thinking logically to solve the given problem or to arrive at a conclusion is known as reasoning.

Reasoning and sequential thinking are examples of mental tools that we use to effectively solve problems or even deal with simple situations.

reasoning: the ability that people have to think and to make sensible judgements can be referred to as reasoning. The reason for something is a fact or situation that explains why it happens or what causes it to happen.

Other useful mental tools are pattern recognition, creativity, imagination, etc. For example, we can use reasoning and creativity to come up with interesting designs. We can also combine simple shapes to create a beautiful design.

Help Abu to make his own pattern. His best friend Ram's birthday is in a few days. Abu wants to make a special greeting card that Ram would love. When thinking about what to draw, Abu gets an idea!

Abu first draws a round shape and colours it red.	
Then, he draws a diamond next to it.	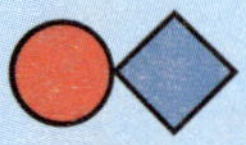
He repeats this till a beautiful pattern is formed.	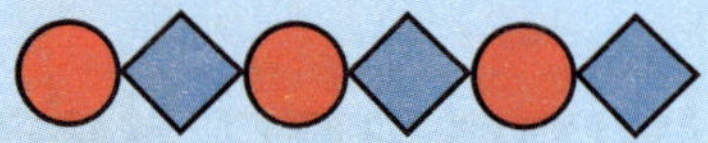
Using simple shapes, Abu was able to make a greeting card that Ram loved!	

Brush up!

Identify the shapes used to make the following patterns and draw them in the given space.

a. 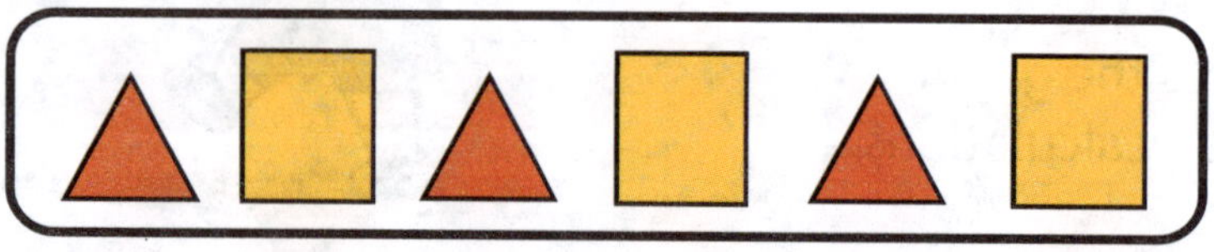

b. 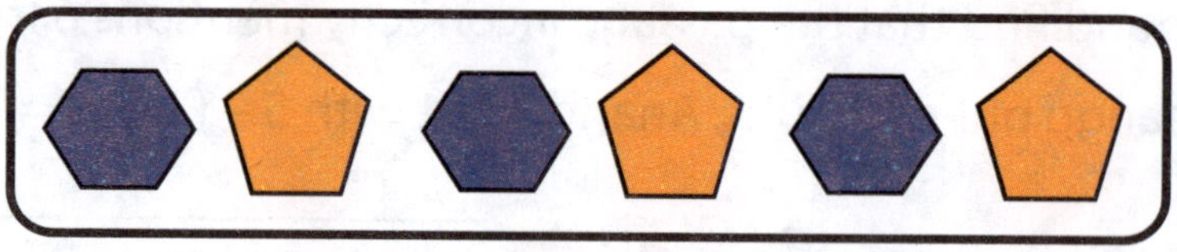

Today I learned!

- Breaking down a task into smaller steps and arriving at possible solutions to achieve the desired goal is known as step-wise thinking.
- After dividing a task into simple steps, it is important to follow the steps in an orderly manner. This is called sequential thinking.
- Reasoning and sequential thinking are examples of mental tools we use to effectively solve problems or even deal with simple situations.

Revise and polish!

1. Cross the odd one out. Give reason for your choice. One has been done for you.

a.

(i) Water ☐ (ii) Milk ☐

(iii) Juice ☐ (iv) Bread ☒

Reason: We drink water, milk and juice. But we eat bread.

b.

(i) Ball ☐ (ii) Earth ☐

(iii) Sun ☐ (iv) Table ☐

Reason: ____

c.

(i) Smartphone ☐ (ii) Shoes ☐

(iii) Tablet ☐ (iv) Laptop ☐

Reason: ____

d.

(i) Cat ☐ (ii) Dog ☐

(iii) Lion ☐ (iv) Whale ☐

Reason: ____

e.

(i) Pencil ☐ (ii) Eraser ☐

(iii) Sharpener ☐ (iv) Chair ☐

Reason: ____

2. Fill in the blanks using the given words.

shapes mental orderly step-wise

a. Breaking down tasks into smaller steps and arriving at possible solutions to achieve the desired goal is known as ____________ thinking.

b. It is important to follow all the steps in an ____________ manner.

c. Reasoning and sequential thinking are examples of ____________ tools.

d. Simple ____________ can be combined to make a design.

3. Fill in the missing terms in the following sequences.

a. BAC DEF BAC ___

b. GHI GHI ___ MNO

c. 11 22 33 ___ 55

d. ___ 234 234 243

e. Green Red Blue Green Red Blue Green Red _____

f. Pink Pink Pink Yellow Yellow Yellow Pink _____ Pink Yellow _____ _____

4. At Ram's birthday party, his friends were playing a game. There are 30 cards mixed in a bowl with a different animal's picture on each card—lion and tiger. The number of cards with each animal is not the same. For example, there could be 16 lion cards and 14 giraffe cards. Within a minute, a group has to count how many lion cards and how many giraffe cards are in the bowl. What is the quickest way to perform this task? Write the solution down in steps.

____

____

Think and Answer

1. Give the routine activities that you do before going to school. What will happen if you change the sequence of activities that you do in the morning?
2. Siya is planning to organize a birthday party for her friend Rakhi. What are the steps that she should follow?

Chapter 7

Features of File Management

After reading this chapter, I will be able to:

- ✔ Explain how to rename a file/folder.
- ✔ Define how to copy or move a file/folder from one location to another.
- ✔ Describe how to delete a file/folder.

Brainstorm and explore!

Fill in the blanks using the given words.

folder   files   extensions   drive

1. Information is stored in a computer in the form of _______________.
2. Different types of files have different _______________ such as .jpg, .mp4, etc.
3. All related files are neatly organized in a _______________ in a computer.
4. The files and folders are further kept in a _______________.

We know that we store all pencils inside a pencil box and that pencil box is kept inside a drawer. Similarly, all files are kept inside a folder and that folder is saved in a drive or another folder.

We already know how to create new files and folders using the **New** option. All files and folders can be accessed through **This PC** icon available on the desktop.

Let us know learn how to rename, copy, move and delete a file/folder.

Renaming a File/Folder

Renaming a file/folder means changing the name of the existing file/folder. It is always better to give a proper name to a file or folder so that it is easy to recognize. For example, all Paint files should be saved with your name or drawing's name and placed in the folder which is under your name. This will make it easy for you to locate your file in a shared computer.

To rename a file/folder, the steps are as follows:

1. Right-click on the file/folder to be renamed and then click on the **Rename** option, as shown in Fig. 7.1.
2. Type the new name and press the **Enter** key.

Remember, no two files can have the same name in the same folder.

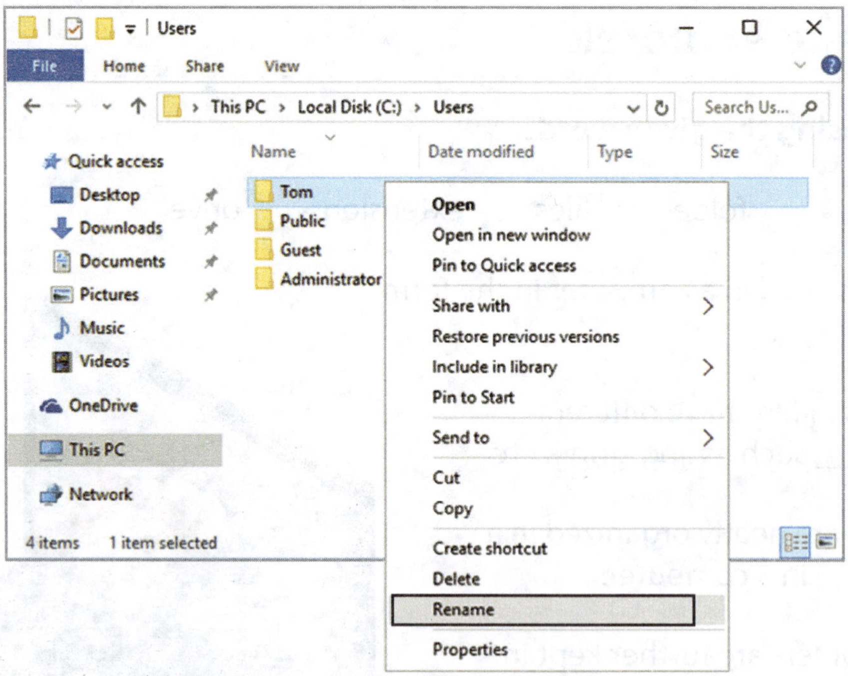

Fig. 7.1 | *Renaming a file/folder*

Apart from renaming a file/folder, we can use right-click to move or copy file/folder to another location (using the Cut and Copy options), delete them, pin them to the Start menu and see their properties.

Technology Literacy

Crank up!

The shortcut to rename a folder/file: select on the folder and press the F2 key.

Copying a File/Folder

Duplicating a particular file or folder is possible using the **Copy** and **Paste** options.

To copy a file or folder, the steps are as follows:

1. Click on the **This PC** icon on the Desktop to find the file or folder that needs to be copied.
2. Select the file or folder that you wish to copy.
3. Right-click on it and select the **Copy** option (Fig. 7.2).
4. Go to the location where this file or folder needs to be placed.
5. Right-click anywhere on the location and select the **Paste** option (Fig. 7.3).

Technology Literacy

Crank up!

Another way to copy a file or folder is by using the keyboard shortcut Ctrl+C, to paste it in the new location, use Ctrl+V.

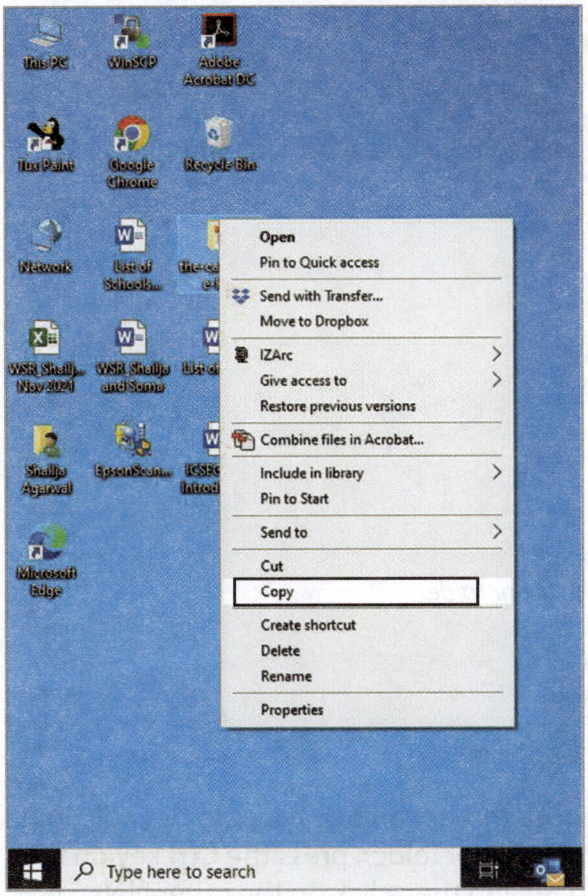

Fig. 7.2 | *Copying a file or folder*

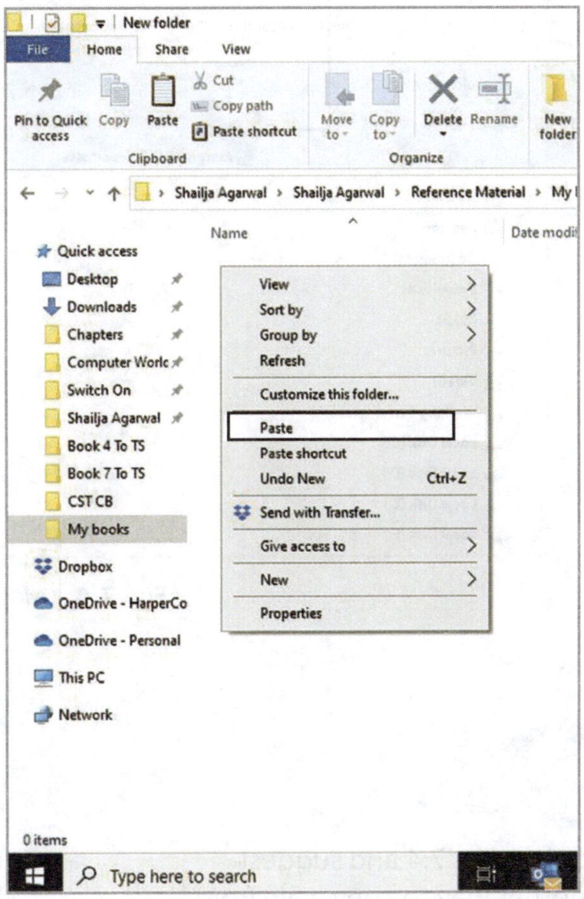

Fig. 7.3 | *Pasting a file or folder*

Moving a File/Folder

Moving a file or folder, moves the entire file or folder to a new location unlike copying the file or folder where another copy is created in a new location (Fig. 7.4).

To move a file or folder, the steps are as follows:

1. Select the file or folder that you want to move.
2. Click on the **Move To** drop-down button under the **Home** tab, in the **Organize** group.
3. Select the destination location where the file or folder needs to be moved.
4. The file or folder would be moved from the source to the destination location.

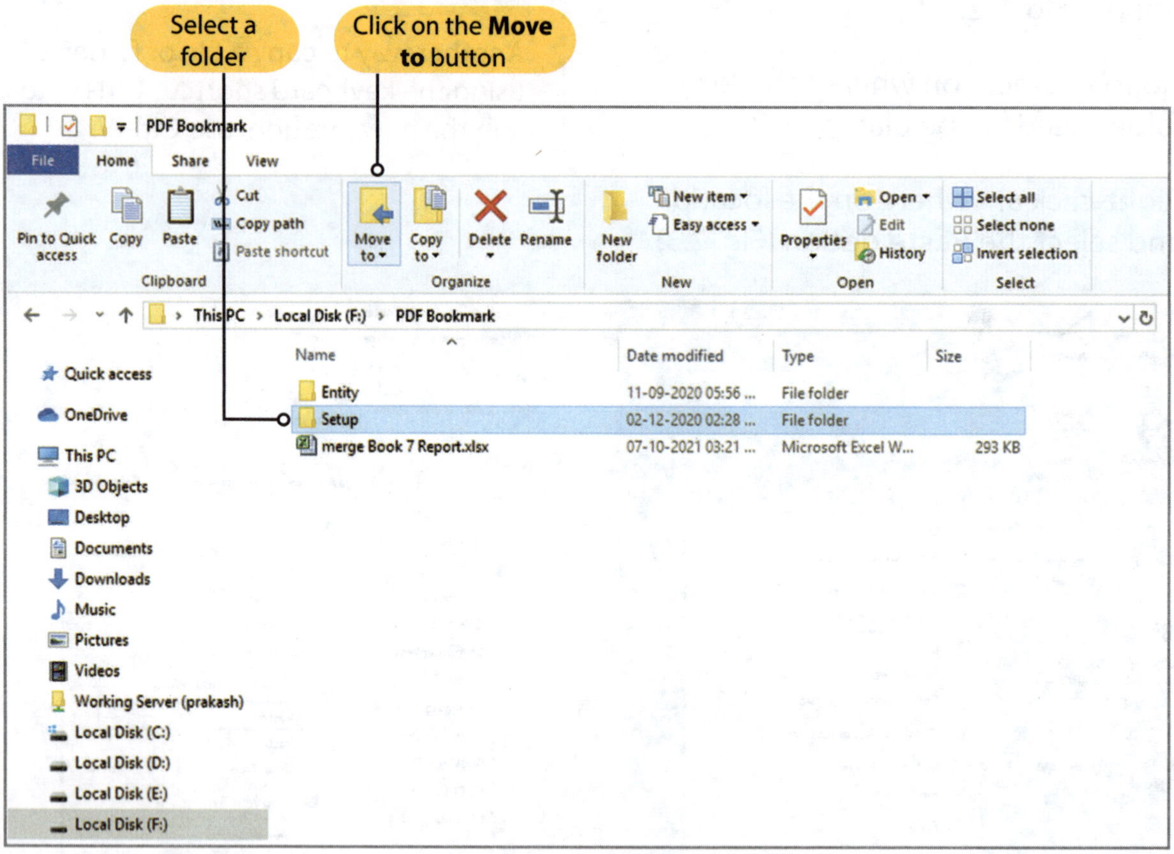

Fig. 7.4 | *Moving the file or folder*

Clear up!

Look at Fig. 7.4 and suggest another way to copy a file from one location to another.

Soak up!

To choose more than one file or folder at a time, click on a file or folder, press the **Ctrl** key on the keyboard and then click on the other file(s) or folder(s) to select them.

Deleting a File/Folder

A file or folder can be removed from the computer using the **Delete** option (Fig. 7.5). There are two ways to do so:

1. Select the required file or folder, right-click on it and select the **Delete** option.
2. Go to the **Organize** group in the **Home** tab and click on the **Delete** button.

A message box will appear to confirm the deletion. Click on the **Yes** to confirm the deletion. This will ensure that the file or folder has moved to the **Recycle Bin** and has removed from the current location. To permanently delete the file from the computer, click on the **Shift+Delete** option or click on the **Delete** drop-down menu and select the **Permanently delete** option.

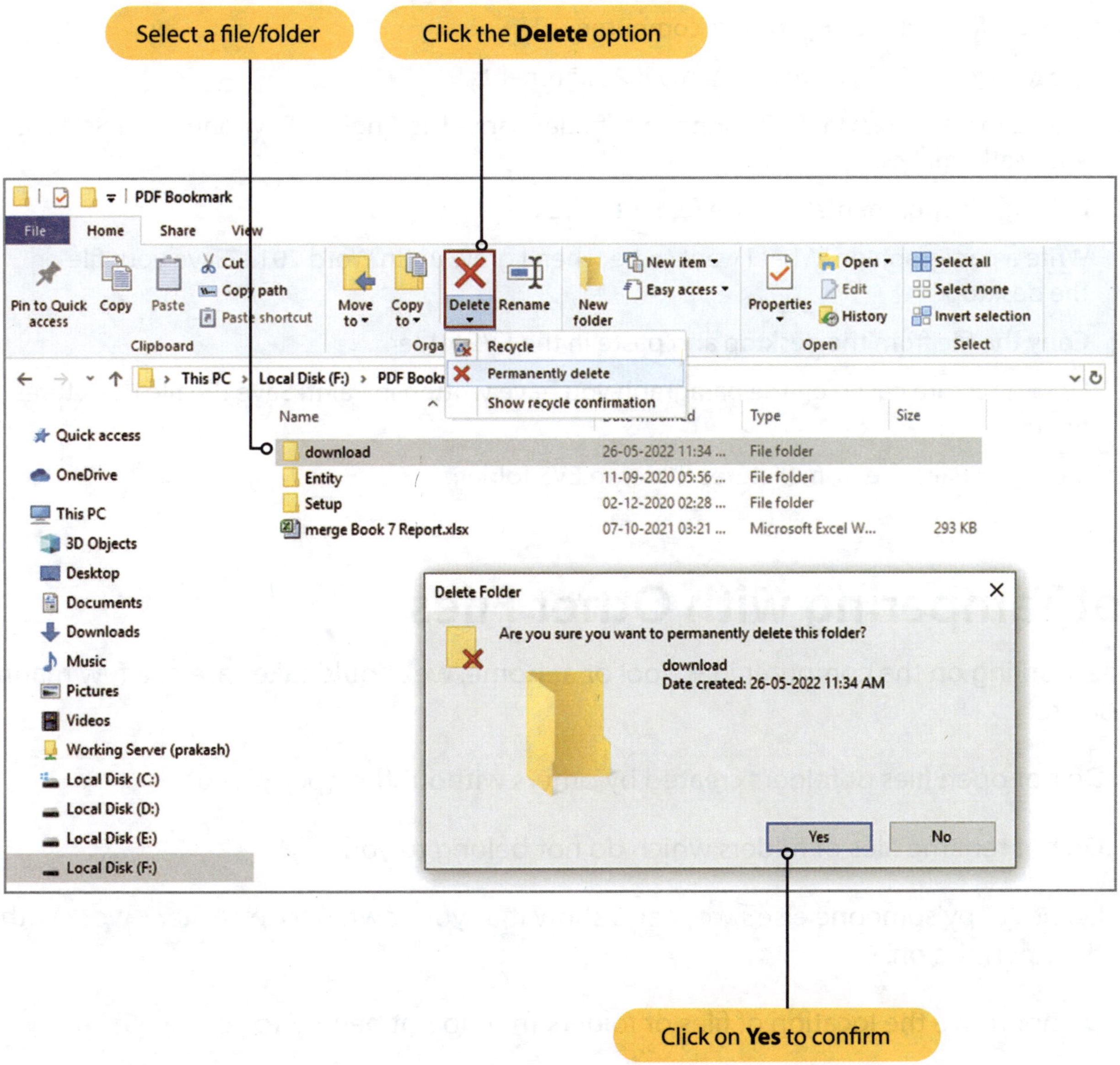

Fig. 7.5 | *Deleting a file/folder*

Soak up!

To remove the deleted file or folder permanently from the computer, go to the **Recycle Bin** and click on the **Empty Recycle Bin** option or press **Shift+Delete** keys. If a file or a folder is deleted by mistake, it can be retrieved from the Recycle Bin. This can be done by going to the Recycle Bin on the desktop, right-clicking on the required file or folder and clicking on the **Restore** option to recover the file to its original location.

Clear up!

Perform the following tasks on your computer.

1. Create a folder in D: drive and name it Assignments.
2. Create three folders in the Assignments folder named as: English, Environmental Science and Mathematics.
3. Rename Environmental Science folder to EVS .
4. Write a paragraph on 'What I want to be when I grow up' in Word 2013. Save your file on the desktop.
5. Copy the file from the desktop and paste in the EVS folder.
6. Draw a picture based on the paragraph you have written in Paint. Save the file in Pictures folder.
7. Move the Paint file from Pictures folder to EVS folder.

Not Tampering with Other Files

While working on the computer in school or at home, we should take care of a few manners. These are:

1. Do not open files or folders created by others without their permission.
2. Do not rename files or folders which do not belong to you.
3. Do not copy someone else's work and show it as your own or copy other's work without their permission.
4. Do not move the location of files or folders that do not belong to you.

Brush up!

Look at the following icons and tick (✔) the icon of Recycle Bin.

a.  ☐

b.  ☐

c.  ☐

Brush up!

Why you should not edit or delete someone else's file/folder?

____

____

____

____

____

____

Today I learned

- Renaming a file or folder means changing the name of the existing file or folder.
- Copying a file or folder means duplicating a particular file or folder.
- A file or folder can be renamed or copied by right-clicking on that file or folder and selecting the Rename or Copy option, respectively.
- Moving a file or folder moves the entire file or folder into a new location. This can be done using the Move to button from the Home tab on the Organize group.
- A file or folder can be removed from the computer by pressing the Delete option.
- While working on a computer that is shared by others, do not tamper with files or folders that have not been created by you by changing their name, content or location.

Revise and polish!

Learning Skills

1. Tick (✓) the correct answer.

a. Priya did not complete her classwork as she was busy playing games in the computer lab. When the teacher moves around the lab to check the work done by the students, she should:

(i) Tell the teacher that she has not done the work. ☐

(ii) Search for her friend's work on the computer and show it to the teacher as her own. ☐

(iii) Move a random assignment into her folder and show it as her own. ☐

(iv) All of these ☐

b. Where do the files move after deletion?

(i) Recycle Bin ☐ (ii) Deletion folder ☐

(iii) Erase Bin ☐ (iv) Deleted files ☐

c. Which of the following options is used to remove a file permanently from the computer?

(i) Delete ☐ (ii) Permanently delete ☐

(iii) Remove ☐ (iv) Permanently remove ☐

d. Which of the following options is clicked to move a file from one location to another?

(i) Move to ☐ (ii) Copy to ☐

(iii) Copy in ☐ (iv) Move in ☐

e. A message box appears when we click on the ______________ button.

(i) Move to ☐ (ii) Copy to ☐

(iii) Delete ☐ (iv) All of these ☐

2. Fill in the blanks using the given words.

Moving permission Rename Shift+Delete Copying

a. To rename a text file on the desktop, click on the ______________ option.

b. One should always open a file created by others after getting their ______________.

c. To delete a particular folder permanently, press ______________ keys.

d. ______________ a file moves the entire file to a new location without duplication.

e. ______________ a file is possible by pressing the Ctrl+C keys on the keyboard.

3. State whether the following statements are true (T) or false (F).

a. You can rename a folder using the Rename option. ☐

b. You can rename two files as "reshmi.doc" in the same folder. ☐

c. Copying of file creates two versions of the same file at different locations. ☐

d. Pasting a folder in new location is done by pressing Ctrl+C keys. ☐

e. You should not move another user's files into your folder. ☐

f. Once created, one cannot change the name of a file or a folder. ☐

4. Write the functions performed by the following keyboard shortcuts.

a. Ctrl+C ____________ b. Ctrl+V ____________

c. Shift+Delete ____________

5. Answer the following questions.

a. Write steps to move a certain file from C: drive to D: drive.

b. How a folder can be renamed?

c. Write any three manners to avoid tampering while using a shared computer.

d. How a file can be removed from the computer?

e. What is the use of Recycle Bin?

Lab Activities

Experiential Learning

Create a folder with your name on the desktop and do as follows:

a. Create a file with your name inside that folder.

b. Move the new file from the folder to the desktop.

c. Delete the folder created.

Think and Answer

Problem-solving | Critical thinking

1. Ekta accidentally deleted a folder from the drive. Is it possible to restore it? If yes, how?

2. Saloni wants to create two folders in different drives with the same name. Can you tell her if it is possible?

3. Ankur wants to delete a file permanently from the computer. Can you help him do so?

Competency-based question

Computational Thinking

Worksheet 1 (Chapters 1 and 2)

1. Match the following data sets to complete the information.

a.	Search "coding classes in India" on search engine	(i)	001
b.	Find your rank in the class	(ii)	1460 search results with different websites of coding classes in India
c.	Testing blood sample of an individual	(iii)	List of scores of all the students
d.	+91 876510**00	(iv)	Finding the blood group of the individual
e.	M Akshay F Sonam Mahima Pooja	(v)	Calling on +91 876510**00 phone number
f.	1 in binary language	(vi)	Akshay Sonam Mahima Pooja (Grouping individuals on the basis of their gender)

2. Which unit of measurement will be used in the following situations?

a. To represent the number 1 __________

b. To store a poem typed using the Notepad application __________

c. To represent the letter Z __________

d. To store big data __________

e. To store an animated 1 hour-long movie __________

f. To check capacity of the latest hard drive with maximum storage capacity __________

g. To store a photo album __________

3. Give the steps for the following.

a. Rita is playing loud music on her computer in the living room. Her mother asks her to lower the volume it as she needs to answer a phone call. Help Rita reduce the volume of the speaker.

b. Sanil goes to his friend's house to complete a project. He boots his laptop to research a few topics but is unable to access the internet. Help him connect to the Wi-Fi.

c. Jayant is looking for a document on his computer but has forgotten the folder's path. Help him search the folder using the Search bar.

d. Priya needs to take the laptop for a 3-hour computer program. How will she ensure that it does not switch off?

e. Chetna accesses a certain folder very often. Help her make a shortcut to this folder on the desktop.

4. **Notice the parts of Windows 10 desktop and draw icons for the following.**

   a. Weak Wi-Fi signal

   b. Microsoft Edge browser

   c. Sound is on mute

   d. MS Word

   e. Folder

Worksheet 2 (Chapters 3 and 4)

Competency-based question

Critical thinking

1. **Imagine you are a journalist and need to write a book review to be published in a newspaper. Write a review on a story book of your choice.**

   Can you type the review using the MS Word application? Which steps will you follow to check spellings and use the Thesaurus?

2. **Write a story using the following words.**

   elephant dolphin birds banyan tree palace mountains

   Can you type this story using the MS Word application? Tick (✓) the MS Word features you can use to format the story.

   a. Underline the nouns used in the story

   b. Left-align the text

   c. Give a title to the story and align it in the centre on top of the document

   d. Set font size of the title to 25 and make it Bold and Italics. Change the font colour to any colour of your choice

   e. Change the casing of the title to 'Capitalize Each Word'

   f. Change the font size of the rest of the text to 12 and font style to Verdana

   g. Set the line spacing to 1.5

   h. Take the printout of the document once complete and read out the story to the class

3. **Write the correct words for the following jumbled words.**

   a. PCORTOOL ____________ b. WDSKYEOR ____________

   c. BWROGSIN ____________ d. WONTERK ____________

   e. RUL ____________

4. Solve the following crossword puzzle.

Across:

1. Web application that helps us search any information
2. This is used in the address bar of the browser
3. These are used to store information of the websites or web pages

Down:

4. A web browser
5. Short form of World Wide Web

5. Answer the following questions.

a. Mitali accidentally closed her internet browser midway while working on an important project. What should she do to open the same webpage she was collecting information from?

b. www.mindchamp.in is a company teaching coding and game designing. What is its domain name?

Can you tell why it is using the above domain name? If they need to change the domain name, which one is most apt for this company?

c. Aditya is completing his project work while listening to music using the web browser. Is it possible? How?

Worksheet 3 (Chapters 5, 6 and 7)

1. Give the steps to make a simple presentation about your favourite food items. In the presentation, include a slide on dividing the food items as healthy or junk.

2. Give the steps for the following activity.

Form a group of three students and make a presentation on "Flags of different countries around the world". Then, show the presentation to all students of your class.

3. Identify whether the following are sequential or not. If yes, highlight the common patterns.

a. abbaabbaabbaabba

b. 12345123123123

c. Aarav Jia Dia Aarav Jia

d. She sells sea shells on sea shore

e. 989898898989

4. **Solve the following puzzle.**

The cost of the watches is varying. The total cost of all the four watches in a column is given at the top of the column.

Can you calculate the cost for each watch?

 = ______________

 = ______________

 = ______________

5. **Give the steps for the following.**

   a. Create a folder in the C: drive on a computer with the name "<<your name>>_grade4"

   b. Move files all the documents in the "MS Word" folder and all presentations in the "PowerPoint" folder.

   c. Copy a folder and paste it on the Desktop.

   d. Rename a folder to "<<Your name>>_grade4_desktop"

6. **Correct the following sentences.**

a. We should open the files of our friends without their permission.

____

b. Rename the folder of your best friend to your name as a prank and tell them later about it.

____

c. It is alright to delete the presentation of your best friend.

____

d. Save all your files on the Desktop of your school computer as and when you create them.

____

e. The Desktop is looking very untidy with multiple files from different students. So, delete all the files to make it look tidy.

____

Additional Worksheet

1. The steps of organizing a birthday party are jumbled up. Arrange the following in a sequential manner by numbering them.

a. Decorate the venue ☐

b. Cutting the cake ☐

c. Inviting all the friends ☐

d. Buying new clothes for the birthday ☐

e. Arranging food and chocolate at the venue ☐

f. Play games/dance at the party ☐

2. Some pictures may look difficult to draw. These can be made simpler using the step-wise approach. Fill in the missing steps in the following drawings.

a. 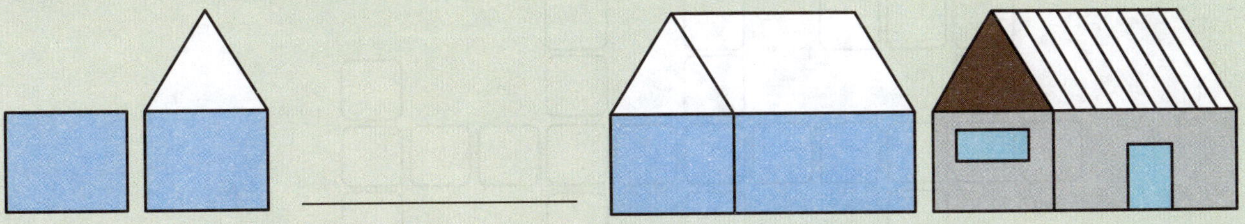

b. 

3. Colour any three balls to get a total of 130.

50 32 45 76 101

28 60 35 67

Fun Activity

Fit all the given words linked to a computer, into the grid. If there is only one word of any length there is only one place where it can go. Look for the clues in the letters you have filled in.

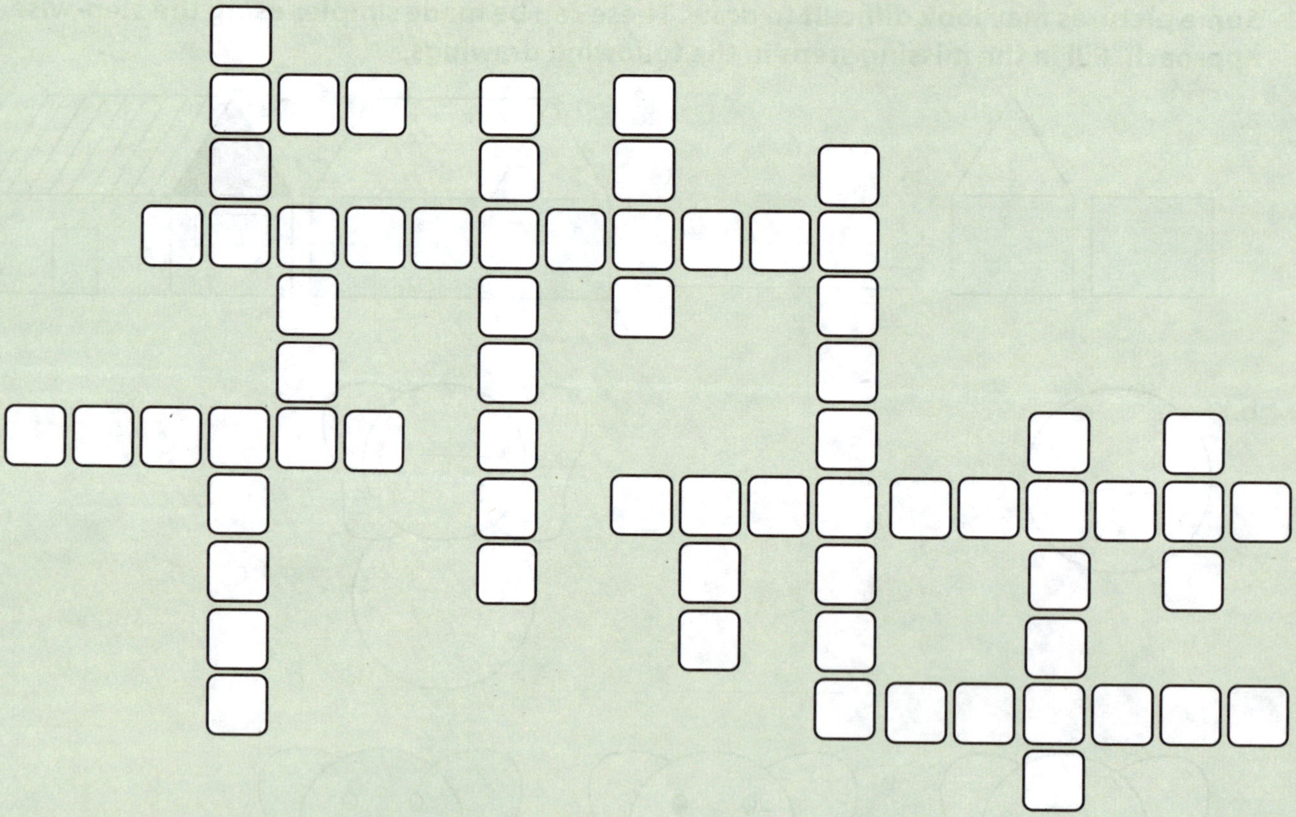

3 letters	4 letters	5 letters	6 letters	7 letters	8 letters	9 letters	10 letters	11 letters
CPU, USB, bit	data, icon, file	drive	folder, memory	storage	computer	analytics	multimedia	information

CLASS

4

QUESTION PAPER SET

A

NCO

SOF NATIONAL CYBER OLYMPIAD 2021-22

DO NOT OPEN THIS BOOKLET UNTIL ASKED TO DO SO

Total Questions: 35 | Time: 1 hr.

Guidelines for the Candidate

1. You will get additional ten minutes to fill up information about yourself on the OMR Sheet, before the start of the exam.
2. Write your **Name, School Code, Class, Roll No.** and **Mobile Number** clearly on the **OMR Sheet** and do not forget to sign it. We will share your marks / result and other information related to SOF exams on your mobile number.
3. The Question Paper comprises three sections:

   Logical Reasoning (5 Questions), **Computers and Information Technology** (25 Questions) and **Achievers Section** (5 Questions).

   Each question in Achievers Section carries 2 marks, whereas all other questions carry one mark each.
4. All questions are compulsory. There is no negative marking. Use of calculator is not permitted.
5. There is only ONE correct answer. Choose only ONE option for an answer.
6. To mark your choice of answers by darkening the circles on the OMR Sheet, use **HB Pencil** or **Blue / Black ball point pen** only. E.g.

   Q.16: _____ means to hold down the left mouse button while you move the mouse pointer to a new place.

   A. Single click B. Double click C. Dragging D. Left click

   As the correct answer is option C, you must darken the circle corresponding to option C on the OMR Sheet. 16. Ⓐ Ⓑ ● Ⓓ
7. Rough work should be done in the blank space provided in this booklet.
8. Return the OMR Sheet to the invigilator at the end of the exam.
9. Please fill in your personal details in the space provided on this page before attempting the paper.

SOF

SCIENCE OLYMPIAD FOUNDATION

Inspiring Young Minds Through Knowledge Olympiads

Name:..

SOF Olympiad Roll No.:.. Contact No.:..

1. Some letters are given which are numbered 1, 2, 3, 4 and 5. Find the combination of numbers so that letters are arranged accordingly to form a meaningful English word.

O	T	N	H	R
1	2	3	4	5

A. 3, 1, 2, 5, 4 B. 3, 1, 5, 2, 4 C. 3, 2, 4, 1, 5 D. 1, 3, 5, 2, 4

2. Find the CORRECT mirror image of the given figure.

A. 

B. 

C. 

D. 

Mirror

3. Which of the following figures will complete the given figure pattern?

A. 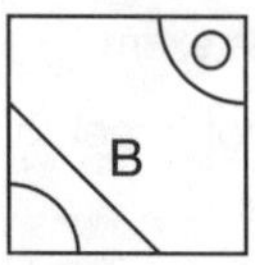

B. 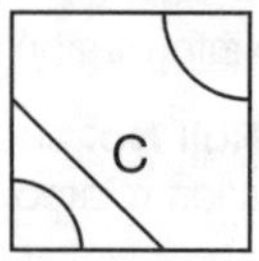

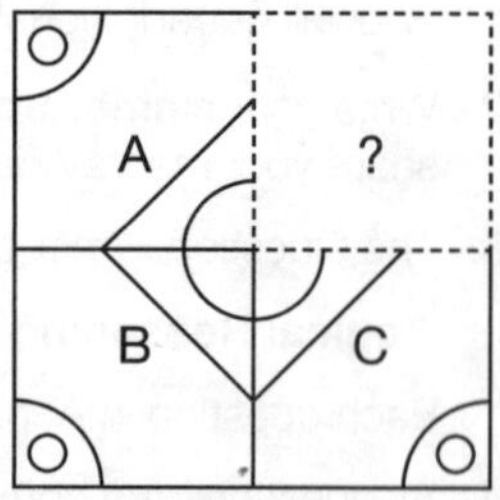

C. 

D. 

4. If the position of cones S and R are interchanged, then cone __________ will be second to the right of fifth cone from the left end.

A. R
B. S
C. X
D. Z

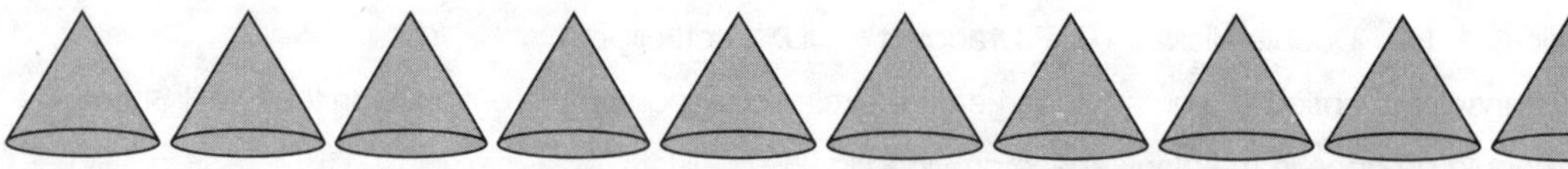

Q X M S P T R L U Z (Right)

5. There is a certain relationship between the figures on the either side of : :. Identify the relationship on the left pair and find the missing figure.

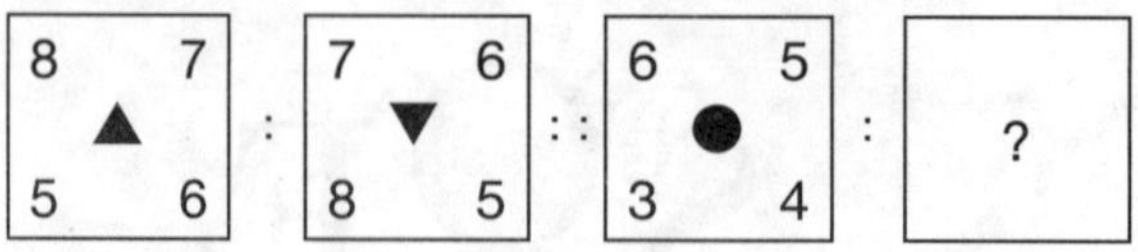

A. 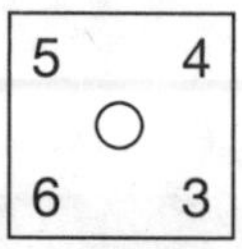

B. 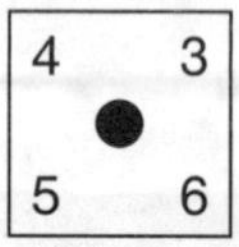

C. 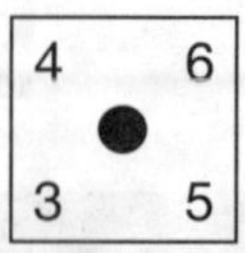

D. 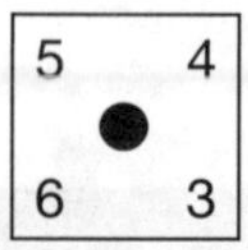

SPACE FOR ROUGH WORK

6. Identify the following.
   - It a manual calculating device.
   - It allows users to represent numbers by the position of beads on the rack.

   A.  B.  C.  D. 

---

7. Which of the following hardware allocates power to the computer?

   A. RAM B. ROM C. Motherboard D. Hard disk

---

8. Which of the following types of software can be considered as a communication software and is used to communicate with your friend staying abroad?

   A. 

   B.  C.  D. 

---

9. What would happen if you select the 'Match case' option given in the Search Options section of Find and Replace dialog box in MS-Word 2010 as shown in the given image?

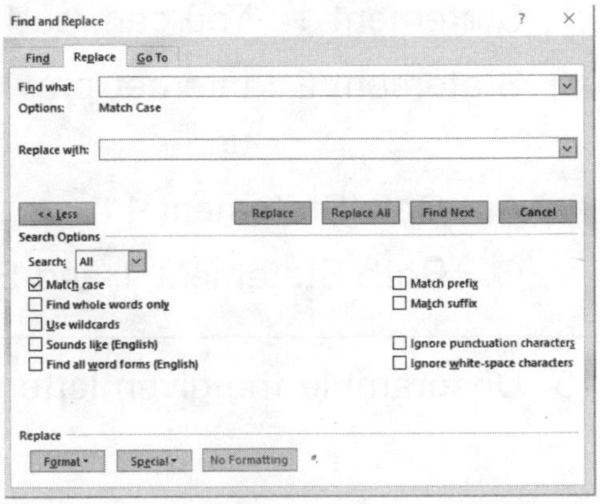

   A. It will perform case-sensitive search.
   B. It will only search words written in bold.
   C. It will only search words that are underlined.
   D. It will only search match prefix.

---

10. Suhana has used the word 'Machine' 50 times in her document. But instead of using the same word 50 times, she wants to use another words with similar meaning in her document. Which of the following options will suggest another word with the same meaning in MS-Word 2010?

   A. 

   B. 
   C. 

   D. 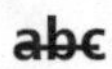

---

11. A humanoid robot is a robot with its body shape built to resemble the human body. Which of the following is an example of such robot?

   A. Sophia B. Alexa C. Cortana D. Siri

SPACE FOR ROUGH WORK

12. Which of the following options of Windows Explorer marked as 1, 2, 3 and 4 can be used as a navigation pane with respect to Windows 7?

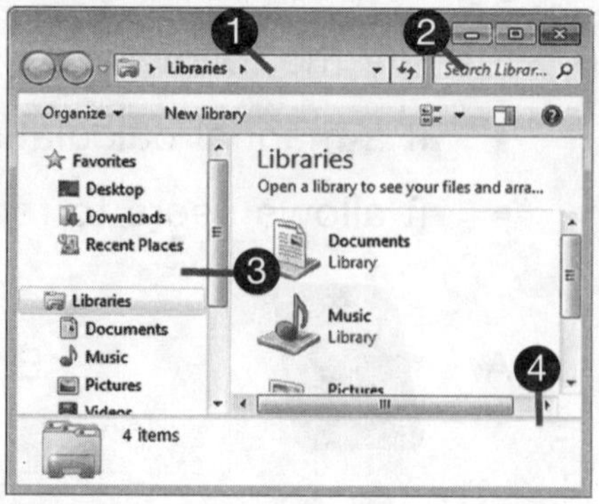

A. 1

B. 2

C. 3

D. 4

---

13. Which of the following options of Windows 7 can be used to do the following tasks?

1. To explore and manage the contents of your computer drive.
2. To check the status of all the storage areas on your computer.

A.  B.  C.  D. 

---

14. Which of the following statements hold(s) true with respect to internet uses?

Statement 1 : You can read electronic newspapers and magazines on the internet.

Statement 2 : Internet provides platforms to stay updated with what is going on around us.

A. Only Statement 1 B. Only Statement 2

C. Both Statement 1 and Statement 2 D. Neither Statement 1 nor Statement 2

---

15. Unscramble the given letters and select the CORRECT statement about it.

EDMOM

A. It represents the first page of any website.

B. It is the device used by ISP (Internet Service Provider) to connect your computer to the internet.

C. It is a type of web browser used to search on internet.

D. It is the area where user enters URL of the website.

---

16. Which of the following types of network is most suitable where business offices are situated at longer distances and they want to communicate with each other easily?

A. PAN B. LAN C. WAN D. CAN

SPACE FOR ROUGH WORK

17. Which of the following operations has been applied on the selected part of the given Image-1 to get the Image-2 as shown here in MS-Paint of Windows 7?

A. 

B. 

C. 

D. 

Image-1

Image-2

18. Which of the following statements is INCORRECT about computer network?
   A. MAN is needed because LAN cannot connect town or cities.
   B. WAN is required to connect countries.
   C. LAN cannot share peripheral devices.
   D. PAN is able to connect devices present within short range.

19. Select odd one out.

A. B. C. D.

20. Which of the following is required to install in your computer in order to work with the physical parts of computer?

A. B. C. D.

21. Which of the following is a service developed by Google, that offers aerial and satellite views of many places?

A. B. C. D.

22. Which of the following jumbled letters is NOT related to the internet?

A. NTEWROK B. OWRSEBR C. EISTEBW D. TERINPR

SPACE FOR ROUGH WORK

23. Identify the given tool with respect to MS-Paint of Windows 7.

A. Airbrush
B. Crayon
C. Natural pencil
D. Watercolor brush

---

24. A device generally found at public places and used for cash withdrawal is known as ___________.

A. Printer
B. Scanner
C. ATM
D. Monitor

---

25. A tiny piece of silicon which has electric circuits on it is called _________.

A. Wafer
B. Chip
C. Bit
D. RAM

---

26. Which of the following is a software?

A. 
B. 

C. 
D. 

---

27. Identify the following.

- It enables sharing of files between teachers and students.
- Documents are stored on Google Drive can be edited in Google Docs.

A. 
B. 
C. 
D. 

---

28. Which of the following options of Windows 7 allows you to swap the functions of the left and right mouse buttons?

A. 
B. 
C. 
D. 

---

29. Which of the following internet services allows your parents to do online transaction with their bank?

A. E-shopping
B. E-banking
C. E-selling
D. E-mailing

SPACE FOR ROUGH WORK

30. Fourth generation of computers were developed using microprocessor technology. Which of the following type of computers are NOT based on this technology?

A.  B.  C.  D. 

ACHIEVERS SECTION

31. Consider the following statements.

1 : You need a pen or pencil to write on a paper.

2 : Our brain controls all the different parts of the body and make them work together.

Which of the following devices is best suitable for performing above mentioned tasks on computer respectively?

A. , 

B. , 

C. , 

D. , 

32. John typed his name in MS-Word 2010. But he is getting red wavy lines under his name. To remove the red wavy lines, what steps he needs to follow?

1. Right click on the name → Select add to dictionary
2. Go to Review tab → select 

option → Click on Add to Dictionary option.
3. Right click on the name → Translate

A. Only 1 B. Both 1 and 2 C. Both 2 and 3 D. Both 1 and 3

33. In the given diagram, devices marked as ❶, ❷ and ❸ are capable of sharing information, hardware devices such as printer and an internet connection within a home. Which of the following types of network is formed here?

A. LAN

B. WAN

C. BAN

D. MAN

SPACE FOR ROUGH WORK

34. Which of the following tools is used in the given drawing of MS-Paint in Windows 7?

A.  B. 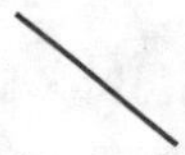 C.  D. 

35. Computer works on an IPO cycle.

X → Y → Z

Input Process Output

Which of the following options can be used as X, Y and Z respectively?

	X	Y	Z
A.	Joystick	CPU	Monitor
B.	Printer	Modem	Scanner
C.	Plotter	CD	Stylus
D.	Digital camera	Headset	Headphones

ANSWER KEYS

1.	(B)	2.	(B)	3.	(D)	4.	(B)	5.	(D)	6.	(B)	7.	(C)
8.	(D)	9.	(A)	10.	(B)	11.	(A)	12.	(C)	13.	(D)	14.	(C)
15.	(B)	16.	(C)	17.	(C)	18.	(C)	19.	(D)	20.	(C)	21.	(A)
22.	(D)	23.	(A)	24.	(C)	25.	(B)	26.	(B)	27.	(C)	28.	(A)
29.	(B)	30.	(C)	31.	(A)	32.	(B)	33.	(A)	34.	(A)	35.	(A)

Techfest Asia's Largest Science & Technology Festival

THE INSTITUTE OF Company Secretaries of India PRESENTS

INTRODUCING

IGKO SOF INTERNATIONAL GENERAL KNOWLEDGE OLYMPIAD

IEO SOF INTERNATIONAL ENGLISH OLYMPIAD

NSO SOF NATIONAL SCIENCE OLYMPIAD

IMO SOF INTERNATIONAL MATHEMATICS OLYMPIAD

NCO SOF NATIONAL CYBER OLYMPIAD

ISSO SOF INTERNATIONAL SOCIAL STUDIES OLYMPIAD

ICO SOF INTERNATIONAL COMMERCE OLYMPIAD

For latest updates & information, please like our Facebook page (www.facebook.com/sofworld) or register on http://www.sofworld.org/subscribe-updates.html

For Level 1 and Level 2 preparation material / free sample papers, please log on to www.mtg.in

SOF SCIENCE OLYMPIAD FOUNDATION

National Office: Plot 99, First Floor, Sector 44 Institutional area, Gurugram -122 003 (HR) India

Email: info@sofworld.org | Website: www.sofworld.org

Regd. Office: 406, Taj Apt., Ring Road, New Delhi-110 029

Note: Please address all communication to the National Office only.